# 4

# ★AVERY PLAYS

## PATRICK DORSEY

**friendly Neighborhood**
PUBLISHING

SAINT LOUIS

ISBN 978-1-939437-33-4

Cover Illustration by Patrick Dorsey.
copyright © 2014 by Friendly Neighborhood Publishing

Manufactured in the United States of America

Friendly Neighborhood Publishing is an imprint of Legendary Planet, LLC
PO Box 440081
Saint Louis, Missouri 63144-0081

LegendaryPlanet.com

Also by Patrick Dorsey

*God's Forge*

*Spirits of St. Louis: Missouri Ghost Stories* (contributor)

*The Champion Sky* (expected 2014)

*For Terri, for welcoming me to tell stories and for indulging my sense of humor for four years;*

*For the Avery players, for all the good times and for taking the characters I put on paper and making them breathe;*

*For the Avery kids and parents, for cheering in the right places and laughing at all the funny parts.*

# CONTENTS

# Taking a Role in The Avery Play

## A Tradition of Fun for More Than Half a Century

*A Calling, Maybe, But Definitely Called*

I BECAME A PART OF THE AVERY PLAY TRADITION when I found myself pressed into writing a "small but funny part" for a would-be Avery player. I'd been a parent of kids attending Avery Elementary in Webster Groves, Missouri for a few years, and had attended a few times the annual play put on by the parents of the school's PTO. The aspiring Avery player had volunteered for the show but was too late to snag one of the small walk-on parts and lacked the considerable time to commit to taking on a lead role.

"Just a little something to squeeze in between some of the other characters in this scene" I was told as I was handed a script, followed by the requirements "And I can't sing or dance or act. But it should be funny!"

Oh, is that all . . .

But I hit upon an idea, and the bit I wrote went over well with the director and ultimately the audience, eliciting laughs throughout. So when the writer of that show and several before it stepped away from the job, I thought I'd take a crack at it. And then I took another crack, and another and another...*Lost at Avery...Steve & Terri's Excellent Avery Play Adventure...Whatever...Shenanigans!* ...It was fun. It was good practice, trying out a different kind of writing in scripting a play. And it was a great opportunity to tell stories and get immediate feedback—an audience, especially an audience full of kids, makes it obvious when they're entertained or bored, tickled or not, and I learned some great lessons in character building, storytelling , and timing. With each play, I found things more familiar and I became more connected to the show and the tradition it represented not just for the school, but for the larger community around it.

*The Avery Play Tradition*

HOSTED BY AVERY ELEMENTARY SCHOOL IN WEBSTER GROVES, MISSOURI, the Avery Play is a decades-old community tradition that stretches back to 1949.

In those postwar years, the American people were anxious about the world around them. Soldiers bearing the scars of the war came home to a country changed by the long years of the planet's first true world war. The destruction and slow rebuilding of Europe, the rise of Communism worldwide, and the at once terrible and wonderful technologies the war unleashed created for America an uncertain world that was as frightening as it was exciting, where each new opportunity presented equally new and intimidating challenges as the world readjusted to an entirely new balance of economic and military power.

In 1949, Harold Downs, principal of Lockwood School felt this, too, and thought the school community needed a lift. Long active in high school and community theatre, he suggested to PTA president Mary Taylor that the school put on "an old-fashioned, down-home play" because "Nothing brings people together like having fun and putting on a show."

Led by that Mickey Rooney-Judy Garland sentiment, on Friday, March 11, 1949, the Lockwood *Showboat* was launched as a community event. It included a parade of decorated cars and parents, teachers, and children. The event included two shows, a raffle, concessions stands, a bake sale, and a "Hall of Wonders."

As reported in the Webster *News-Times*:

> "Swamped by more than 1200 parents, teachers, pupils, and friends of Lockwood School, the Lockwood *Showboat* almost floundered for want of seating space . . . when some 800 persons crowded into the small auditorium for two performances to enjoy one of the most entertaining evenings in the history of the school."

Two more performances were added on Thursday, March 24, 1949 to accommodate the unexpected demand.

A great tradition was born.

Nearby Avery School began holding its own shows in the fall of 1951, encouraged by new principal Edmund Detering, who would became the target of many jokes and parodies in the plays performed during his tenure.

With both schools having plays during the 1950s and early 1960, there was there was strong cross-community support for the two shows—the Lockwood families would attend and enjoy Avery's show in the fall, and the Avery parents would have fun at the Lockwood show in the spring. That community tradition ended sadly in 1966 after Mr. and Mrs. Arch Dickerson and Mr. and Mrs. John L. Lees, the key movers and shakers behind the Avery shows for many years, died in a car accident returning from a football game in Columbia, Missouri. The enthusiasm, drive, and fun behind the Avery shows seemed to pass on with them, and the Avery stage went dark.

The spring shows at Lockwood school continued. And when Lockwood and Avery merged in 1979, the Avery gym once more filled with singers, dancers, musicians, and good and bad jokes. The reborn Avery Show—today known as the Avery Play— has continued ever since, even with every missed cue, forgotten line, or stumbled step, carrying on the tradition of bringing the entire school community—parents and students, educators and staff, friends and family—together.

*Becoming "The Writer"*

THE SHOW WAS GOING STRONG WHEN I JOINED THE AVERY PLAYERS, and my sillier, cartoonier, more self-referential, never-pass-on-a-joke approach to he plays—though different from f previous years—resulted in shows that were liked and well-attended. Beyond the opportunity to see stories I wrote come to life, I enjoyed the fun and flattery of other Avery players I might bump into dropping off in the morning or at the grocery store, as they told me about how much fun they'd had in a part or asked about my plans for the next show. It seemed I had become the Avery Play's designated writer.

But after three spring shows, I found my youngest was in her last year at Avery. Now, there's no hard and fast rule that says once a player has no kids at Avery, they're out. In fact, many alums of the play do come back when a bit part or a stage hand is needed—the call goes out, and it's always answered.

I'd heard of no one else inquiring about writing the play, but still, I wrote it with an eye toward that production being my last. I'd taken small walk-in roles in previous shows, but for this, I added the extra dimension of writing in a character specifically for myself—a character named simply "The Writer"—for an ongoing gag that played out with the other characters throughout the show.

I was on stage after the curtain call of that spring's last performance, shaking hands and accepting too-kind compliments from parents from the audience and cast, and I was thinking already about the next year's show. It would be different, writing as a parent with no kids at Avery to quiz for teacher names or other details to drop in for the Avery students in the audience. Then a fellow made his way through the crowd and introduced himself to me. He told me he was new to Avery and worked with the kids in the afterschool program. He was so charmed, he said, by not just the spirit of community theatre the Avery Play showed but by the script, with its style of an old Hollywood comedy and the ongoing references throughout to those old movies, that he wanted to be sure to express how much he enjoyed it all. The night's performance inspired him, he told me, to jump in and volunteer to be part of the next year's show.

"The Avery play can always use the help," I told him, leading him to meet our producer/director. "What do you do?"

"I'm a filmmaker," he said. "And a writer."

The Avery Play had found its next writer, and in that moment, I went from being The Writer to becoming a link in the show's long and vibrant past.

Talk about becoming part of the tradition. I just didn't think It would happen that fast.

*A Few Things About the Plays*

THE PLAYS PRESENTED IN *4 AVERY PLAYS* ARE THE ONES I WROTE in my tenure as The Writer. They're silly, family-friendly, and meant to be performed by amateurs on the slimmest budget to kids and parents who are having a night out of fun together. My hope is that other groups —schools, churches, community groups—in search of a play to perform for a fundraiser or just to put on a show will find a script here that tickles their funnybone and their creativity.

Some of the jokes, you'll find, are very specific to Avery—teacher names, locations, things going on in the community, the school itself—feel free to change them to fit your school or organization.

There were also set "rules' to what had to be in and Avery Play:

★ Small but memorable parts for three or so teachers in the first scene

★ A small part for the school district superintendent in the first scene

★ A good-natured Kirkwood put-down joke (Kirkwood being the longstanding rival school to Webster Groves, where Avery Elementary is located)

★ At least two musical numbers  (typically set up as one all-moms number and one all-dads number)

★ A small but memorable part for the Avery principal, usually toward the end of the second act

For best effect, please substitute your own principal or teacher or rival school names (in these scripts, I've used generic names for the principal and superintendent.).  And when it comes to suggested musical numbers, they can be incorporated or not (they're never essential to the plot) or you can find your own songs that fit as a segue. Just be sure you've secured all permissions necessary for your performance.

Typically, my Avery Plays featured four lead actors and a variety of back-up characters. This was very much on purpose, not just for storytelling, but for the practical reason that most people are busy and can't commit to large roles. But a small part they can learn quickly, walk on stage, and get a laugh in—that's a role interested parents may make space in a full schedules for.  Plus, these small walk-ons are written so they don't affect the story and can be lifted out easily or their lines combined with another character's if finding cast members becomes a problem.

I'll also confess to a somewhat subversive (others would call it troublemaking) streak that led to occasional...*naughtiness* slipping into a scene or two in each script I wrote. Like the great Warner Brothers animated shorts of the 1930s and 1940s, I reasoned that these plays weren't just for kids and that we could count on a fair percentage of adults in the audience every show. So like the classic cartoons, some jokes were written with those adults in mind and are meant to go over the kids' heads and be caught by the parents. I felt highly praised to have one dad tell me out of the blue how much he liked the "Bugs Bunny" material that I worked in for the adults. But I know some jokes aren't appropriate to everyone, and they're written to lift out of the script easily. Take 'em out if they don't work for you,

And, please, if you do decide to perform one of these Avery Plays, let me know about your show! Tell me your stories about how you staged it or what kinds of changes you made, and what happened backstage and at your performances. Send me pictures—or better yet, a DVD of the production. I can be reached at *PTDorsey@LegendaryPlanet.com* and I'd love to see how others interpret the plays!

I hope you have as much fun performing them as we did!

PATRICK DORSEY
("The Writer")
Webster Groves—February, 2014

# 4
# AVERY PLAYS

LOST
AT AVERY

# Lost at Avery (2008)

*Avery Elementary needs a new gym!*

*When Martha, America's favorite celebrity designer, is teamed with Bob, kids' favorite TV builder, the new gym project seems destined for stellar success. But when the site's mysteriously wrecked by night, they have to team up with tool-expert parent Tim and plucky bilingual explorer girl Dora to get to the bottom of the mystery.*

*A lost key and a secret door lead them on an adventure that takes them to the strange and kooky underworld beneath the school where they must race to finish construction before the kids return in the fall—and somehow avoid getting LOST AT AVERY.*

LOST AT AVERY WAS MY FIRST TIME OUT as a writer for the Avery Play. Although I was fairly confident as a writer and storyteller, the learning curve was still steep. The collaboration process was new to me (really, most writers are used to working odd hours, tucked in a corner alone—and like it that way), and I had to learn the limits of what will work on the budget and skills of a PTO grade school parents' play.

I learned that maybe collaborating form the beginning wasn't the best way to build a coherent script quickly. Too much input left me juggling too many elements. And as the new guy, I really wanted to be helpful and accommodating, especially following in the footsteps of s longtime writer known for being exacting with her material. Don't get me wrong—a lot of great ideas came out of the script meetings in the director's living room. And still more developed on set as scenes were blocked out and rehearsed. But there were elements I had to drop from the tale I had in my head in order to fit everything else, and I perhaps could have kept them—and ended up with a more integrated final play—if I'd presented a more complete story up front.

I also learned the importance of keeping the story structure at least somewhat "modular" —the School Superintendent gag from the opening scene of the next year's play, *Steve & Terri's Excellent Avery Play Adventure*? That was written and rehearsed for *Lost at Avery*, but cut at the last minute when the superintendent had to drop out of his appearance to meet another commitment. In productions like these, you need to allow that someone may become suddenly unavailable.

Like most of the Avery Plays I'd seen before, this one is a mash-up of parody characters the kids would find familiar—only for this story, I added a few that were more to be recognized by the parents in the audience. One |fun element for the kids that year was that Avery Elementary was actually going through a substantial construction project to put in a new gym. The ongoing loss of playground space to construction equipment and the ongoing rearranging of classrooms as construction moved through the building were regular parts of all the Avery students' school year for some time—a perfect springboard for a device to draw the kids into the story.

All Spanish phrases in the dialogue are presented phonetically in the script for those who picked another language
to study in school. My best advice in staging this show: Get the greatest height difference you can between your Martha and Dora actresses. For the Avery production, our Dora was about five feet tall, and our Martha almost six (and then wore heels!). The contrast really sold the two characters in their opening scenes and put the audience squarely into our strange Avery world. And, however long you want to make Dora's pauses, make them longer. Painfully longer. Trust me on that.

So, up first: my playwriting debut with the Avery Play, a silly quest by mismatched, confused characters quibbling their way through a magical, imaginary land in the strange tunnels beneath the school—*Lost at Avery.*

"LOST AT AVERY"


Written by

*Patrick Dorsey*

## "LOST AT AVERY"

CHARACTERS:


BOB, the builder put in charge of the Avery expansion project because of his construction skills and way with the kids.

MARTHA, celebrity designer, sentenced to live at Avery over the summer and help guide the project -- she wears a big, fat, flashing house arrest bracelet on her ankle.

TIM, local parent and construction know-it-all who grunts frequently and makes things collapse or explode even more frequently.

DORA, plucky bilingual explorer girl, lost in the bowels of Avery since her show was cancelled.

TEACHERS, elementary educators anxious for summer break.

BUD, CHICO, CURLEY, and other CONSTRUCTION WORKERS, the guys putting up the new gym.

MRS. CRUMBTOPPING, MRS. CAKEMIX, MRS. CLAMCHOWDER, and other PARENTS, because every school has them.

BOSS LOOMPA, ASSISTANT LOOMPA, and other assorted LOOMPA-LOOMPAS, little orange people like Oompa-Loompas, but different.

DR. DOE, a school district superintendent.

DR.SMITH, a school principal.

LUNCH TRUCK LADY, driver of a cantina truck who tempts the construction crew with her goodies and double entendres.

THE MUMMY, linen-wrapped for freshness.

THE PHANTOM OF THE OPERA, masked and haunting the shadows with his songs.

<u>"LOST AT AVERY"</u>

ACT ONE


SCENE 1:

The outside of Avery Elementary. The school building is under construction. A group of CONSTRUCTION WORKERS are setting up, hammering, sawing, etc. as a group of 2-4 TEACHERS Mosey by, ogling the men and giving their thumbs-up.

                    TEACHER 1
        I sure do <u>love</u> the new construction.

                    TEACHER 2
        Me too . . . I'm almost sorry it's summer
        break.

                    TEACHER 3
        I'm looking forward to it. I'm going to
        <u>travel</u>.

                    TEACHER 1
        Where?

                    TEACHER 3
        London, Paris, Rio. Or Branson . . . Or
        Festus.

                    TEACHER 2
        I'm gonna spend my whole summer planted in
        front of the TV and eating Doritos 'til my
        face turns orange.

                    TEACHER 1
        I hope they can at least get all these
        candy wrappers cleaned up . . .

As the teachers drift aside, the Construction Workers go into their STOMP number.



MUSICAL NUMBER:

"Stomp" Routine

A dance performance using buckets, hammers, trash cans, etc. to make music and keep rhythm.

As the number wraps up, one of the Construction Workers gets knocked in the head in a bit of slapstick and falls to the floor. He doesn't get up.

BOB, the builder in charge, enters, unrolling plans.

> BOB
>
> Hey, it's not nap time yet! Get back to
> work!

The unconscious construction worker jumps up and goes back to hammering. The teachers scatter and exit.

> BOB (CONT'D)
>
> We've got a lot to do if we're going to get
> the new gym finished and fixed up before
> summer's over. Can we fix it?

> CONSTRUCTION WORKERS
>
> Yes we can!

Bob looks around, confused. He turns to the audience.

> BOB (CONT'D)
>
> I said, "Can we fix it?"

> EVERYONE
>
> Yes we can!

> BOB
>
> Okay everyone -- I've talked to the boss,
> and we're going to make this the best
> school gym ever! I was thinking we could
> add some tire swings, and a ball pit, and
> maybe a waterslide and swimming pool . . .

MARTHA enters. Put-together, she's fashionable, uncertain but not nervous hey, she's a celebrity -- wearing a giant, flashing house arrest bracelet on one ankle and carrying a decorated, handled basket of pine cones over one arm. She spots Bob, who's clearly in charge.

> MARTHA
>
> Hello, I'm Martha --

> BOB
>
> Glad to meet you! I'm Bob, the builder they
> hired --

He offers his hand eagerly, to shake.

> MARTHA
> (Offers her hand formally)
> Mr. Thebuilder.

                    BOB
Call me Bob.

                    MARTHA
            (Choking on it)
Bob. I was told I'm to report for a special
design project . . . ?

                    BOB
Hey! You're the designer the boss just told
me about! He says you're super-duper, and
we only got you as part of a special deal.

                    MARTHA
Yes . . . community service was part of the
sentence.

                    BOB
I like sentences. Putting words together
with punctuation -- it's almost like
building!

                    MARTHA
Ye-e-sss . . . so what kind of a project is
this?

                    BOB
We're doing an addition --

                    MARTHA
Of course. This is a very small building.

                    BOB
You think so?

                    MARTHA
This is someone's summer cottage, I assume?
Just a tiny place for getting away on the
weekends?

                    BOB
It's a school!

                    MARTHA
A what?

                    BOB
A public elementary school.

                    MARTHA
Hang on . . . I'm a designer and a
celebrity, and I'm not following . . . A
school, you say? Is it like a house, then?

> BOB
> Yes. It's just like a house. Except no one
> actually lives there. But it gets filled up
> every day with people --

> MARTHA
> Like a hotel?

> BOB
> But they don't sleep there. The people are
> kids called students. They show up every
> day, go to a particular room, sit down, and
> learn from their teachers.

> MARTHA
> Like a studio audience! Stu-dio . . . stu-
> dents -- yes, I can hear how the words are
> similar. What kind of show do they tape
> here?

> BOB
> It's a grade school. There's no taping --

> MARTHA
> They do their show live? -- Oh, very
> daring! I'm not familiar with a "grade
> school" show, but I've done my share of
> live spots! I'm certain I can work
> something out to spruce the place up.
> Candles bring romance and warmth to any
> setting, and you'd be amazed how versatile
> pine cones and fabric remnants can be.

She begins gathering pine cones.

Behind her, TIM THE TOOL DUDE enters, in a tie and toolbelt,
inspecting the construction site, getting in the way of the Workers
while they work -- they have to squeeze past him, trip over him while
he's leaning over their shoulders to get a better look, reaching for
tools and equipment while he's handling and inspecting them.

Tim starts re-positioning/hammering one part.

> TIM
> No, no, no -- you need to brace it like
> this --

The structure collapses. Tim shakes his head, jabs a thumb in the
direction of the workman, disappointed and unimpressed.

Bob notices the commotion and darts over.

                    BOB
Uh, hi? Can I help you?

                    TIM
No, no. Just helping out the crew here.

                    BOB
Uh, thanks. Listen, we don't mind people
watching, but we ask that the public stays
over there --

                    TIM
Oh, I'm not the public. I'm an Avery
parent. Just moved to the neighborhood with
our three boys, and I want to make sure the
gym addition will be as good as it can be.
Have you thought about tire swings?

                    BOB
I just suggested them to Dr. Doe!

                    TIM
Ball pit?

                    BOB
That too!

Behind them, Martha gathers some of the crew. She sits them all on
the ground, handing each a sheet of paper and instructing them on
folding them.

                    BOB (CONT'D)
Say, you seem pretty handy.

                    TIM
I know my way around tools. My name's
Tim --

                    BOB
          (Shaking his hand)
Bob. The builder the school hired to --

                    TIM
-- But most people call me . . . Tool Dude!
Ah-ah-ah!

Tim spies two of the crew plugging in some large, elaborate power
saw.

                    TIM (CONT'D)
Is that a Binford 40 amp with a variable-
speed, dual-torque, high-compression, drop-
forged --

                        BOB
          You bet it is! We just got it. Top of the
          line for cutting --

                        TIM
          It's adequate.

                        BOB
          Adequate?

                        TIM
          Yeah. To be outstanding, it needs one
          thing.

                        BOB
          What's that?

                        TIM
               (Drawing a screwdriver from his belt)
          MORE POWER!

He pushes the Workers aside, goes to work on the saw. After a few
seconds of grabbing parts and tossing parts aside, he whirls to show
the new, improved tool, which shines in his hand like the sword
Excalibur.

He hands it confidently to the crewman he took it from.

                        TIM (CONT'D)
          Fire it up!

The construction guy plugs it in, turns it on, starts cutting.

                        CONSTRUCTION WORKER
          It cuts just like before.

                        TIM
          There's a new switch on the side -- dial it
          up to eleven.

He dials it up. Lights dim, and there's a godawful shriek as he puts
it to the wood and it flies from his hand, skittering across the
stage and off.

                        BOB
          I hope it doesn't make it to the street --

They watch in fear, reacting to it as it races off unseen. There's an
awful grinding sound.

                        BOB (CONT'D)
          I think that's Dr. Smith' car --

                        TIM
          He probably needed new tires, anyway.

                    BOB
          And a new bumper.

                    TIM
          Hey you kids, look out!

There's another awful grinding sound.

                    TIM (CONT'D)
          He probably wanted a new bike anyway --

                    BOB
          And new shoes, I hope. Say, Tim --

                    TIM
          Tool Dude --

                    BOB
           -- Tool Dude, I've got someone you can
          help over here.

He starts to walk him over to Martha.

                    TIM
          Sorry fellas, but it looks like someone
          else needs a little assistance from the
          Tool Dude --

They snort.

                    BOB
          And I thought Spud made things difficult at
          job sites.

Martha sees them, stands up to greet Tim.

                    MARTHA
          Hello, I'm Martha --

                    TIM
          Tim. But you can call me Tool Dude.

                    MARTHA
          Tim it is.

                    BOB
          What do you have my guys working on over
          here?

                    MARTHA
          We're making some decorations --

                    BOB
          It's a construction site.

                    MARTHA
          -- which doesn't mean it can't be cozy or
          convey a certain style or charm. We're
          taking ordinary sheets of newspaper, and
          applying the wondrous secrets of the
          ancient Japanese art of origami,
          transforming them into these delightful
          suns --

She holds up an incredibly elaborate sun that no one could possibly
make by folding paper.

                    MARTHA (CONT'D)
          -- after only 192 simple steps. Everyone,
          show Mr. Thebuilder -- what we've done so
          far.

One worker holds his up. It's a lop-sided take on Martha's perfect
one

The next holds up his proudly. It's a balled up wad of newspaper.

                    MARTHA (CONT'D)
          I don't think you quite got the starting
          folds right on that one.

Another holds up his. Just as elaborate as Martha's, it looks like
running horse.

Martha, Bob, and Tim all do a double-take.

                    MARTHA (CONT'D)
          Not the project we were doing, but very
          accomplished nonetheless.

                    TIM
          So you're decorating the new addition?

                    MARTHA
          Bringing personal touches, style, and
          warmth to the setting.

                    TIM
          What kind of budget do you have?

                    MARTHA
          Budget?

                    TIM
          Yeah, how big a budget did they give you to
          work with?

                    MARTHA
I'm sorry, I'm a wealthy celebrity
designer, and this is both my first
construction project and my first project
in a "school", so I'm a little unfamiliar
with all the terminology.

                    TIM
Are you kiddin' me?

                    MARTHA
Budget . . budge-it?
          (Spots one of the guys working
           with a crow bar)
Budge-it? Is it a tool for moving things?

                    BOB
It helps you spend money.

                    MARTHA
Oh, that I know how to do -- you send your
assistant out with your gold card. Is that
another term for an assistant? It sounds
like a word for a cute little bird "here
budgie, budgie, budget, here -- "

                    BOB
I should've gone to the Bahamas with Wendy
and Spud --

A horn sounds, and all the construction crew begins packing their
stuff up.

                    BOB (CONT'D)
Quittin' time!

                    TIM
Already?

                    MARTHA
My, how time flies!

                    BOB
The day can go pretty quick when you need
to move the story along and get to the next
scene.
          (To the crew as they file off)
See you tomorrow morning, guys! First
thing!

Everyone exits but Bob and Martha. Bob rolls up his plans and
starts off. Martha looks a little panicked.

                    MARTHA
Mr. Thebuilder --

                    BOB
Yes?

                    MARTHA
I wanted to confirm my accommodations --

                    BOB
Your what?

                    MARTHA
Where I'm staying.

                    BOB
Wherever you want.

                    MARTHA
No, according to the, uh, terms--
        (Points discreetly to her ankle band)
-- I have to stay on the premises until the
project's complete.

                    BOB
Oh, right. Dr. Smith told me something
about that. He said if you asked, I should
tell you to go into the school through that
door and turn right.

                    MARTHA
And that's where I'll find my suite of
rooms?

                    BOB
Sorry, I think that's Muck calling me!

                    MARTHA
I didn't hear -- ?

                    BOB
        (Leaving)
Can't keep a big red bulldozer waiting!
Don't want him going all "Maximum
Overdrive" on us while he's watching
Pilchard!

                    MARTHA
You said that door?

                    BOB
See you in the morning!

Bob exits.

Alone, Martha pauses, then goes into the school. She returns with a sleeping bag and cooler, both covered in thick dust.

>                    MARTHA
>           That is not a suite!

She pops out a cell phone.

>                    MARTHA (CONT'D)
>           And, of course, no signal. How am I
>           supposed to call the front desk and get
>           this all taken care of?

She paces.

>                    MARTHA (CONT'D)
>           I can't stay here for the night! It's
>           too . . . non-cozy, un-pretty, anti-
>           charming.

She looks at the band on her ankle, then to a point at the edge of the stage.

>                    MARTHA (CONT'D)
>           I'm sure there's some leeway --

She starts for the edge of the stage, looks all around her --

>                    MARTHA (CONT'D)
>           I'll just take a bit of a walk, see if I
>           can find anyplace else to --

She carefully starts to set a foot offstage --

A PIERCING HORN BLASTS. She startles crazily, darts back to center stage in a bit of funny physicality.

Slowly, she creeps back to the edge of the stage.

Cautiously, she inches her foot closer to the edge, flicks it over and back --

The horn blasts. Martha frowns.

>                    MARTHA (CONT'D)
>           -- or maybe I can stay here. Fix things up
>           a bit. Yes! Some cute valances, a -- a rich
>           table runner and a whimsical centerpiece
>           for the desk I saw in there --

She paces, anxious and uncertain.

>                    MARTHA (CONT'D)
>           -- nothing says "welcome" like some
>           homemade paper luminaries lining the walk.
>           Perhaps a topiary . . .

And she goes in the building.

Two PARENTS, MRS. CRUMBTOPPING and MRS. CAKEMIX, each walking a PLUSH DOG ON A LEASH, wander by as Martha disappears into the school. They stop and Mrs. Cakemix points at the building.

> MRS. CRUMBTOPPING
> (To the toy dog on the leash)
> Sit.

Mrs. Crumbtopping jerks on the leash and the dog falls over.

> MRS. CRUMBTOPPING (CONT'D)
> Good dog, Sparky.

> MRS. CAKEMIX
> I tell you, Mrs. Crumbtopping, the place is haunted.

> MRS. CRUMBTOPPING
> Oh, come on, Mrs. Cakemix.

> MRS. CAKEMIX
> I saw it just the other day! Explain to me then why the kids all ran screaming from the building in the middle of the afternoon, and no one's been back since!

> MRS. CRUMBTOPPING
> Because school let out for the summer?

> MRS. CAKEMIX
> (Beat) That makes sense. But even during school, whenever you and I walk by with the dogs in the evening, no one ever goes in, no one ever comes out.

> MRS. CRUMBTOPPING
> 'Cuz it's nighttime, and they close grade schools at night --

> MRS. CAKEMIX
> Oh, I've seen things --

> MRS. CRUMBTOPPING
> I bet you have.

> MRS. CAKEMIX
> Mysterious lights, and crashes and banging.

> MRS. CRUMBTOPPING
> Betty Crocker-Cakemix! You know better than that --

The school lights up mysteriously and there are crashes and bangs.

Mrs. Crumbtopping's creeped out, and starts tugging on the dog's leash.

>                    MRS. CRUMBTOPPING
>          C-come on, Sparky.

Mrs. Crumbtopping exits, dragging the dog behind.

>                    MRS. CAKEMIX
>          Up the airy mountain, down the rushy glen,
>          we daren't go a-hunting, for fear of little
>          men --

Candy wrappers are pitched from the building and land by Parent 2, who skitters off.

>                                           END SCENE 1.

SCENE 2:

Inside an Avery classroom, Martha's remaking the space into a jarring cross between third grade classroom and designer show space.

>                    MARTHA
>          An arrangement of miniature daffodils and
>          purple hyacinth can add a touch of cheerful
>          color to any space.

She looks around the room, trying to make herself believe it.

>                    MARTHA (CONT'D)
>          At least it's better than all the alphabets
>          and number lines and
>          maps -- so PBS!

Behind her, a small door opens and a wad of candy wrappers is chucked into the middle of the floor. Martha turns as the door closes quickly. Suddenly irritated, she stomps over.

>                    MARTHA (CONT'D)
>          How many of these candy wrappers can they
>          leave littering up this place?

She snatches them up, marches them over to the decorated trash can.

>                    MARTHA (CONT'D)
>          Of course, no one probably noticed the
>          litter basket when it was all drab green.
>                    (Admiring her handiwork)
>          Now that I've decoupaged it in with
>          reclaimed Sally Foster wrapping paper
>          scraps, it's a real treasure.

Among the wrappers, she finds a large, oversized, brass key.

> MARTHA (CONT'D)
> How curious and delightful -- I know just
> the place for such a charming antique
> key . . . I bet it goes to that cute little
> door in the corner!

She tries it. It doesn't open. She tries the key, and the door creaks open.

> MARTHA (CONT'D)
> A dark, forbidding tunnel twisting deep
> down into the gloom behind it.
> > (Aside)
> Obviously the perfect place to go look for
> craft supplies.

She starts down the tunnel, and the door slams shut behind her. Startled. She drops the key. Now panicked, she dashes back to the door, tries it.

> MARTHA (CONT'D)
> Locked!?!

She pounds on the door with no effect.

> MARTHA (CONT'D)
> If only I had one of those budge-its the
> men were using earlier!

She continues into the darkness. The floor is covered in candy wrappers, like a Webster street with leaves in the fall.

> MARTHA (CONT'D)
> Honestly, who eats this much candy?

She hunts around, patting her hands on the floor, the walls.

As she reaches one particular spot, DORA pops out from behind some boxes.

> DORA
> ¡Hola! (O-lah)

Martha screams.

Dora screams.

They both scream, then take turns screaming.

They both jump and scream until each realizes the other means no harm.

> MARTHA
> Hello, I'm Martha --

DORA

I'm Dora. Dora the --

MARTHA

Where are we?

DORA

This is the dungeon. Every school has one!

MARTHA

What are you doing down here? How long have you been here?

DORA

*¡No se! (No say)* We were in the middle of making one of my shows, and while I was checking my map, the director got a phone call. I heard him say something about being cancelled, and when I looked up from the map, everyone was gone!

MARTHA

Yes, that's how they treat you when your show's cancelled. Or when your SEC filings aren't all in order. So, Nora --

DORA

Dora!

MARTHA

Dora -- I had a key that opens that door at the end of the tunnel. But I dropped it, and now --

DORA

You need help finding the key?

MARTHA

Yes, that would be --

DORA
(To the audience)
Can you help us find the key?

Martha looks around, unsure who Dora is speaking to.

DORA (CONT'D)
(To the audience)
Great!
(To Martha)
I'll need your help to get into my backpack to find the map!

                    MARTHA
You have a map? Let's see if there's
another way out!

                    DORA
Say Backpack!

                    MARTHA
Excuse me?

                    DORA
Say Backpack!

                    MARTHA
Can't you just take the map out?

                    DORA
Say Backpack!

                    MARTHA
I mean, it's right there! I can see it
sticking out under the flap --

                    DORA
Say Backpack!

                    MARTHA
          (Mumbling, annoyed)
Backpack.

                    DORA
Louder!

                    MARTHA
          (Hysterical)
BACKPACK!!

Dora reaches around and pulls her rolled-up map from her backpack.

                    DORA
Let's see -- According to the map, we have
to go through the Hallway of Gold Stars,
head through the Tunnel of Cafeteria
Mayhem, and then take a left at the
Teacher's Lounge Double-Secret
Refrigerator --

                    MARTHA
We have to go all that way?

                    DORA
        That's what's on the map! Say it with me:
        Hallway of Gold Stars, Tunnel of Cafeteria
        Mayhem, Teacher's Lounge Double-Secret
        Refrigerator!

                    MARTHA
        You could try using your indoor voice
        occasionally, dear.

                    DORA
        Say it with me: Hallway of Gold Stars,
        Tunnel of Cafeteria Mayhem, Teacher's
        Lounge Double-Secret Refrigerator!

                    MARTHA/DORA
        Hallway of Gold Stars, Tunnel of Cafeteria
        Mayhem, Teacher's Lounge Double-Secret
        Refrigerator!

                    DORA
        Great! Let's go -- ¡Vamonos! (Bah-mo-nos)

She starts off. Martha follows, hesitant, then stops.

                    MARTHA
        What would you possibly find at a Teacher's
        Lounge Double-Secret Refrigerator?

                    DORA
        Two grape sodas and a peach Nehi -- it says
        so right here on the map!

She starts off again, singing.

                    MARTHA
        So it does . . . Listen, Aurora --

                    DORA
        Dora!

                    MARTHA
        -- Dora, I'm fairly sure I dropped the key
        over there. I don't think I got as far as
        this when I found it missing --

Something scurries behind them and giggles. Martha looks over her
shoulder, and hurries to catch up with Dora, who doesn't seem to
notice.

                    MARTHA (CONT'D)
        Aren't we there yet?

                    DORA
          Nope! We haven't even crossed el *Rio de
          Cucarachas!*

                    MARTHA
          The what?

                    DORA
          ¡El Rio de Cucarachas!

                    MARTHA
          I apologize, but I studied <u>French</u> when I
          was younger -- it's snootier.

                    DORA
          *El Rio de Cucarachas* -- the River of
          Cockroaches!

                    MARTHA
          Ewwwwwww!

She jumps up on something.

                    DORA
          Don't be silly! We're not there, yet!

                    MARTHA
          You never mentioned that.

                    DORA
          I only list the three main landmarks.

                    MARTHA
          You may want to <u>revisit</u> that policy. How
          will we get across?

                    DORA
          There's vines to swing across, a log to
          climb across, or tortoises to hop across.

                    MARTHA
          What if I fall in?

Dora waves and wiggles her fingers right in Martha's face, like crazy
bug legs. Martha whips her face away, disgusted, and waves them off.

                    MARTHA (CONT'D)
          I'm not going there at all! Cafeteria
          mayhem and a double secret refrigerator
          were one thing, but roaches -- well, they
          have no distinction or refinement, they're
          neither warm nor homey, and they're the
          opposite of charming and stylish! They're,
          they're <u>nega-charming</u> and <u>dis-stylish</u>!

                    DORA
But we need to work together to find the
key!

                    MARTHA
I'm a celebrity, and I don't have to work
with anyone!
          (Reconsiders)
-- Except as directed by the court. Thank
you, Laura --

                    DORA
Dora!

                    MARTHA
-- Dora. The biggest problem I've had since
I arrived is that I haven't been doing
things my may. And that the way that's
always worked out best for me!

Martha stomps off, and trips, falling flat on her face --

-- where she finds the key!

                    MARTHA
The key!

She runs to the door.

                    MARTHA (CONT'D)
Come on, Flora --

                    DORA!
Dora!

                    MARTHA
-- Dora! We're going out this door and
getting out of this dungeon!

                    DORA
But what about our adventure?

                    MARTHA
I have the key! We don't any adventure now!

                    DORA
But what about all the fun we'd have? And
the things we'd learn along the way?

Martha opens the door.

                    MARTHA
We don't need to do any of that now. And I
can get back to work, finish this "school"
project and --

She turns back. Dora's disappeared.

                        MARTHA (CONT'D)
            Hellooo?

Silence.

There's a crash, then another, sounds of things collapsing and breaking. Martha jumps. She slams the door, and dives under her dusty sleeping bag, wrapping it tight over her head so only her face shows.

Shivering, her eyes dart all around, until she finally begins to nod off and falls asleep.

As she lays there, the skittering figures from the corners walk out into the stage and are revealed to be LOOMPA-LOOMPAS.

They circle Martha curiously, and then begin to chant and sing:

                        LOOMPA-LOOMPAS
            Loompa-Loompa, doompity-dee
            How do you get two sides to agree?
            Loompa-Loompa, doompity-day
            When everyone wants to have their own way?

And they march off.

                                        END SCENE 2.


SCENE 3

Morning. Martha is curled up under her sleeping bag, snoring loudly with her mouth wide open. She and everything around her are covered in candy wrappers.

Bob enters.

                        BOB
            Martha?

                        MARTHA
                (Mostly asleep, dismissing him)
            Eggs Florentine and the duck crepes . . .

                        BOB
            Lady, I don't even have cereal and pop-
            tarts.

Martha blinks sleepily, confused, then recognizes Bob

                        MARTHA
            Oh . . . Mr. Thebuilder. I thought you were
            my waitstaff.

                        BOB
            Your what?

> MARTHA
> They seem oddly late.

> BOB
> There shouldn't be anybody here besides
> you . . . but that's what I came to talk to
> you about.

She gets up. All the wrappers slink off her. She looks around,
exasperated.

> BOB (CONT'D)
> You like candy much?

> MARTHA
> I don't know where these all keep coming
> from.

She leans on a desk, drawing her hand slowly away as she finds a
tennis-ball-sized wad of gum stuck to her hand.

She shakes it, trying to get it off, but it holds fast to her
fingers.

She tries wiping it back on the desk, but it still doesn't come off.

> BOB
> Oh, you're a gum chewer.

> MARTHA
> I certainly am not --

Martha grabs up one of the wrappers, and with exaggerated effort,
peels the wad off her hand.

> MARTHA (CONT'D)
> -- and were I, I'd dispose of it properly,
> wrapping it even in the least charming
> paper scrap and disposing of it in the
> nearest litter receptacle.

She does this.

> MARTHA (CONT'D)
> Refuse we can all live with.
> (Brushing her fingers, straightening her hair,
> outfit)
> Now, you said you had something to ask me?

> BOB
> Yes --

                    MARTHA
          Good, because, last night, I had some of
          the strangest dreams. But somehow, they've
          left me inspired, and I find myself
          awakened and overflowing with ideas and
          concepts.

                    BOB
          I'm very much looking forward to all of
          them, too . . .

He leads her outside --

                    BOB (CONT'D)
          But what I'd really like to know is, what
          happened?

The construction area is wrecked. Almost nothing is still standing,
tools and wood strewn all about. The Construction Crew is at work
picking things up. Tim and some Parents are standing nearby, shaking
heads, pointing, and talking amongst themselves.

                    MARTHA
          Oh my word . . . .

                    BOB
          I haven't seen anything this bad since that
          night Muck and Scoop got into the high-
          octane gasoline.

Tim drifts away from the group, looking over the destruction up-
close.

                    MARTHA
          Who could have done something like this?

Tim drifts closer to her and Bob.

                    BOB
          I don't know who could have done something
          like this. I'd like to think it was an
          accident.

                    MARTHA
          One would have to be a tremendous boob to
          do this kind of damage accidentally.

Unwitting, Tim has edged between Bob and Martha.

                    MARTHA (CONT'D)
          But who could be that big a boob?

                    BOB
          And do this kind of damage?

Tim looks up at them suddenly realizing.

                    TIM
              (Grunting a confused "not me!")
          Uh-aoooh?!?

They just stare at him, accusing.

                    TIM (CONT'D)
          Ohhh, no. Wasn't me. I was in my neighbor's
          yard all night.

They're not buying it.

                    TIM (CONT'D)
          You can ask him when he stops by to give me
          the, uh, estimate for replacing his picture
          window. And the half of his deck nearest my
          house . . .

                    BOB
              (To Martha)
          Well, did you see anything last night?

                    MARTHA
          N-noo . . . it was dark and I was --
              (Indicates her ankle band)
          --inside for the night.

                    BOB
          Did you hear anything?

                    MARTHA
          There was some crashing. But it was dark,
          and I was having these very strange dreams.

                    BOB
          Maybe there's a clue in them. Why don't you
          come over here and tell me about them, and
          we'll see what we can figure out.

They drift offstage, pausing as they pass Bud, Chico, and Curley.

                    BOB (CONT'D)
          Oh, my three new assistants.

                    BUD
          We've finished looking it over.

                    CHICO
          Yeah . . . it's wrecked.

                    BUD
          Of course he knows it's wrecked.

>                    CURLEY
>          Then what's he askin' for?

>                    BOB
>          Never mind that. Now, boys, how long's it
>          going to take?

Bud unrolls a large sheet of building plans.

>                    BUD
>          It's gonna put us a week behind, maybe two.

>                    BOB
>          Oh no! Our schedule was tight already,
>          losing two weeks -- I don't know if we'll
>          be able to have the addition ready in time
>          for all the kids!

>                    BUD
>          Don't you worry, chief. We're like the
>          genies of the lamp, the three of us! We'll
>          get this sorted out in no time!

>                    BOB
>          That's the spirit! I like you fellas more
>          already! Can we fix it?

>                    BUD/CHICO
>          Yes we can!

>                    CURLEY
>                 (Shrugging)
>          I'm thinkin' maybe . . . it kinda
>          depends --

Bob, Martha, and Tim exit.

The Construction Crew begin working, Curley picking up a long board and hefting it over his shoulder.

He turns, nearly hitting Bud, who bends over to pick up a hammer as the board swipes over him.

Chico actually sees it and ducks.

>                    BUD
>          Watch where you swing that thing!

Curley turns back to him, swinging the board again --

>                    CHICO
>          Waddaya mean?

-- which this time, connects with Bud.

The slapstick bit continues, a series of near misses, proceeding to accidental smacking, hammering, and general getting knocked around with boards, hammers, ladders, rakes, ropes, hoses or whatever.

Other construction workers enter, carrying supplies, tools, just kind of working their way into the scene.

> BUD
> What are they going to do about all this mud when we're done?

> CHICO
> Plant grass, I guess.

> CURLEY
> How?

> CHICO
> Sodding would be expensive, so I'd guess seed.

> BUD
> Grass seed?

> CHICO
> What other kind?

> CURLEY
> I planted bird seed once.

> BUD
> What grew from that?

> CURLEY
> Birds. (Beat) Problem was, I didn't know what to feed them after that . . .

> CHICO
> Anyone know what time it is? It's gotta be close to noon.

> CURLEY
> Knock, knock!

> CHICO
> Who's there?

> CURLEY
> Jamaica.

> CHICO
> Jamaica who?

> CURLEY
> Jamaica my lunch yet? I'm starvin'!

A peppy horn sounds, someone honking to get attention. Some of the crew sigh in resignation, others look up in fear.

>                    BUD
>          D'oohhh . . . it's the Lunch Truck Lady!

Chico picks up a lunch box.

>                    CHICO
>          I brought today! I'm outta here!

He sprints off, vaulting a sawhorse to escape.

>                    CURLEY
>          It wouldn't be so bad if her food wasn't
>          so . . . Bleecchh . . .

>                    BUD
>          I'd be happy if she just sold the lunches
>          from inside her truck and didn't come out
>          and hang around to bug us . . .

>                    CURLEY
>          Bugs! You think that's what she puts in the
>          food?

They knock it off quickly as the LUNCH TRUCK LADY slinks up to them, in her diner uniform and apron. Her hands hiding something behind her back, her hair up in a hairnet, she's clearly there for more than selling lunch to hungry men . . .

>                    LUNCH TRUCK LADY
>          Hello, boys!

>                    CONSTRUCTION WORKERS (ALL)
>          Hello Lunch Truck Lady.

>                    LUNCH TRUCK LADY
>          What's anyone in the mood for today?

>                    BUD
>          Uh, lunch?

>                    LUNCH TRUCK LADY
>          Then maybe you'd like to have a look at my
>          melons --

She draws one hand from behind her back, revealing a cantaloupe.

>                    LUNCH TRUCK LADY (CONT'D)
>          -- or try the muffin --

She draws the other hand from behind her back, revealing an oversized blueberry muffin.

                    BUD
Oooh, blueberry!

              LUNCH TRUCK LADY
Or you can indulge in my sweet potato
pie . . .

She nods back toward the truck offstage. The guys don't get it.

                    BUD
What do you recommend?

              LUNCH TRUCK LADY
I always like meat . . .

                  CURLEY
I like peanut butter.

              LUNCH TRUCK LADY
          (Throwing up her hands, giving up)
Of course you do.

                    BUD
That sounds good to me, too. Peanut butter
and grape jelly. On white bread.

                  CURLEY
With the crusts cut off!

              LUNCH TRUCK LADY
Just the way your mom used to make 'em.

                  CURLEY
Used to? The way she still does! Mom's the
best.

                    BUD
Yeah!
          (Aside)
Aren't moms the best?

(If no applause follows, our plants in the audience start it.)

Shaking her head, Lunch Truck Lady exits. The Construction Workers
all break for lunch as Bob, Tim, and Martha enter, Tim and Martha
each with large coffee cups.

Bob picks up the plans his crew was working from, rolling them up.

Tim takes a big swig from his cup and does a spit take.

                    TIM
Gyahh -- this coffee's terrible!

                    BOB
          I made it this morning . . . what's wrong
          with it?

                    TIM
          It tastes like mud.

                    BOB
          You bet -- it's <u>fresh</u> <u>ground</u>!

Bob grins, waits for the laugh, Tim glaring. He looks to Martha. She
rolls her eyes and tosses her cup away.

                    BOB (CONT'D)
          Wow, that one always goes over big with all
          the earth-movers on a site . . .

                    MARTHA
          Oh, before it gets too late, I wanted to
          speak with you about my accommodations.

                    BOB
          I'm really not in charge of that.

                    MARTHA
          Certainly you can do <u>something</u>? I mean, my
          room doesn't even have a walk-in closet.

                    TIM
          Any closet's a walk-in if you try hard
          enough.

They notice a groups of PARENTS crowded near the sign showing the new
school, milling impatiently.

                    BOB
          Uh-oh.

                    TIM
          What is it?

                    BOB
          Parents.

                    TIM
          Schools are usually full of 'em.

                    MARTHA
          I thought they had a studio audience?

                    BOB
          That's <u>students</u>.

                    MARTHA
          Of course.

                    TIM
What's the problem with the parents?

                    BOB
When you've worked on as many of these
school construction and expansion projects
as I have, it's just . . .

                    TIM
Oh, they can't be that bad --

              MRS. CRUMBTOPPING
They call that a font? I'd never pick that
for a school sign.

              MRS. CAKEMIX
They should make the windows taller, let
the light in.

              MRS. CRUMBTOPPING
And the landscaping . . . it looks like a
playground. They need something beautiful.

                    MARTHA
That's my cue if I ever heard it.

                    BOB
Wait --

                    MARTHA
Why?

                    BOB
              (Grim, fearful)
Let's just say, when they're in a group
like that . . . I've seen parents do things
even a parent wouldn't do . . .

                    TIM
What's that mean?

                    BOB
              (To Martha)
It means be careful.

Martha approaches the parents

                    MARTHA
Hello, I'm Martha --

She strays too near the edge of the stage, and the air horn blasts.
Everyone on stage jumps, startled while Martha hides her annoyance.

              MRS. CRUMBTOPPING
Are you in charge here?

                         MARTHA
              I'm in charge --

The parents move toward her, circling, cutting her off like a pack of
wild dogs.

She'd suddenly menaced by the parents.

                         MARTHA (CONT'D)
              -- of the design and decoration. You need
              to talk with Mr. Thebuilder over there.

They turn to Bob. He realizes he's clutching the rolled-up plans in
his hand, and tries to quickly hide them behind his back.

                         MRS. CRUMBTOPPING
              You're the builder?

Bob nods, smiles weakly.

                         MRS. CRUMBTOPPING (CONT'D)
              And those are your plans?

                         BOB
              Yes.

                         MRS. CRUMBTOPPING
              So you think you have a plan, do you
              builder?

                         BOB
              I do have a plan.

                         MRS. CRUMBTOPPING
              I bet you have a plan. A planny plan, I'm
              sure, builder!

                         BOB
              Yes.

                         MRS. CRUMBTOPPING
              A plan in your hand, A plan of your own, is
              it? Builder?

                         BOB
              It's the approved plan, that the boss --

                         MRS. CRUMBTOPPING
              But he's not here. It's just you and me and
              your plan, isn't it, builder?

Bob makes a run for it, dropping his plan.

The parents give chase.

                    MRS. CRUMBTOPPING (CONT'D)
          We think the brick should be laid in a
          different pattern!

                    MRS. CAKEMIX
          And the building shouldn't be so
          rectangular!

                    MRS. CLAMCHOWDER
          We love the building the way it was! Can't
          the addition look just like the old
          trailer?

Martha wipes her brow -- that was a close one.

Tim saunters over to where Bob was standing, casually scoops up the
plans, and sidles nonchalantly next to Martha.

                    TIM
          You know, I have some ideas about these
          plans, too.

                    MARTHA
          As do I.

Tim pulls a pair of big markers from his tool belt and hands one to
Martha.

Like a couple of Kindergarteners, they start drawing <u>all</u> <u>over</u> the
plans.

                    MARTHA (CONT'D)
          We can apply a more Baroque line to the
          exterior silhouette, lending a more
          classical --

                    TIM
          Ah -uh-uh -- need a bigger breaker box,
          more outlets . . . higher ceilings --

                    MARTHA
          What for?

                    TIM
          Ceilings are never high enough -- Trust me,
          anywhere I go, things are always crashing
          into 'em.

                    MARTHA
          Niches --

                    TIM
          Wire conduit --

                        MARTHA
          Crown molding --

                         TIM
          Self-shovelling sidewalks --

                      MARTHA/TIM
          Pocket doors --

                         TIM
          Automatic, <u>powered</u> ones, like on *Star Trek*!
          Ooh -ah-ah!

Bob staggers back into the scene, glancing over his shoulder.

                      TIM (CONT'D)
          Bob! You okay?

Martha stashes the plans behind her back, starts rolling them up as
Tim goes to Bob's side.

                         BOB
          Sure am! Just took a little maneuvering to
          get away. Next time, they'll know better
          than to chase a builder with a talking
          steam roller!
                    (Calling OS)
          You show 'em Roley!

                       ROLEY (OS)
          Rock 'n Roll, Bob!

A truck horn sounds in the distance.

Martha sidesteps them, slides over and drops the plans back where Bob
left them.

                         BOB
          I sure am glad to have you two helping me!

                         TIM
          Thanks, Bob.

                        MARTHA
          Yes, thank you.

                         BOB
          No need to thank me. I'm just really,
          really grateful I have you two working with
          me. Lots of people, like those parents,
          want everything exactly their way.

> BOB (CONT'D)
> They insist on making a project fit what
> they want, without any regard for the
> project or the people it's for or the
> people doing the work. Sometimes, they act
> like those parents that chased me.
> Sometimes, they're sneaky about it.

Martha and Tim look embarrassed.

> BOB (CONT'D)
> But you two -- you have terrific skills and
> great ideas, but you don't try to force
> them.

Martha and Tim share a shamed glance.

> BOB (CONT'D)
> In fact, I think that might be what
> happened here last night.

> TIM
> You do?

> BOB
> Someone was unhappy with what we're doing,
> so they tore it all down.

> MARTHA
> But you'll just put it back up. They'd have
> to know that.

> BOB
> People don't always make sense when it
> comes to things they don't like or don't
> want.

> TIM
> Wow, look at the time. I'll be late for --

> MARTHA
> And I need to get back to work on the swags
> and finials I was planning --

> BOB
> Wait -- if you two have just a minute --

> TIM
> Sure.

> MARTHA
> Absolutely.

                         BOB
          Martha, tell me about your dream last
          night.


                                        END SCENE 3.


SCENE 4:

Night. Martha, Tim, and Bob are in Martha's classroom, with
flashlights and light-up headgear, Tim with an elaborate light up
miner's helmet.

Martha and Bob just stare at it, Bob points, speechless.

                         TIM
          Built it myself.

                         MARTHA
          As I would have guessed.

                         TIM
               (To Martha)
          I still can't believe you left a little
          girl locked in a dark dungeon.

                         MARTHA
          It was a dream! Haven't you ever done
          anything weird in a dream?

                         TIM
          Like showing up for school in Mickey Mouse
          ears without your pants and realizing
          there's a test you haven't studied for?

                         BOB
          Who hasn't had that one?
               (To Martha)
          You said you were dreaming about the
          crashes outside, and they turned out to be
          real.

                         MARTHA
          Yes, but the other one, with that little
          girl --

                         BOB
          I can't help thinking there's something to
          it, especially since the other one turned
          out to have happened for real.

                         MARTHA
          But it was just a dream! A crazy, silly --

>            TIM
> Is this the key you used to open the door?

>            MARTHA
> Well, yes, but perhaps I saw it while I was
> sprucing up, and it stuck in my mind --

>            BOB
> Is this the door?

>            MARTHA
> It looks something like the one from my
> dream, but doors are typical imagery that
> Freud identified as an archetypal --

Tim and Bob are watching her, confused.

>            MARTHA (CONT'D)
> Oh, open the door already.

Bob opens the door.

>            MARTHA (CONT'D)
> With a dark, forbidding tunnel twisting
> deep down into the gloom behind it.

>            BOB
> Let's go!

Led by Bob, they all proceed through the door.

Once they're all on the other side, Martha looks up suddenly, whirls
to Tim, the last one through.

>            MARTHA
> Wait! Make sure you block the door with
> something, otherwise it will --

It slams shut as before. Tim rattles the handle, throws himself
against it, to no good.

>            TIM
> Owwwww . . . this is just like my
> anniversary.

>            MARTHA
> How's that?

>            TIM
> Well, my wife and I were talking about all
> our years being married, and I told her
> that I'm just like a fine wine . . . I only
> get better with age.

                    BOB
And?

                    TIM
That night she locked me in the cellar.
(Beat) Of course, maybe that had more to do
with when she was trying on new jeans that
afternoon.

                    BOB
What happened?

                    TIM
She asked me if this one pair made her back
side look like the back side of our house.

                    MARTHA
What did you tell her?

                    TIM
I said, "Of course not --

                    MARTHA
Good.

                    TIM
-- the back of the house isn't anything
close to that color blue."

Dora pops up again.

                    DORA
¡Hola! (O-lah)

Tim and Bob scream.

                    MARTHA
Zora!

                    DORA
Dora!

                    TIM
Everything Martha said really did happen
last night!

                    BOB
Hey, I know you -- Your show used to be on
after mine in the afternoon! Say, where's
Boots?

                    DORA
          (Nervous)
¿Quien? (Kee-en)

                    BOB
          That little monkey that always followed you
          around.

A spotlight flashes on a pair of EMPTY RED BOOTS in the corner, one
tipped over.

                    DORA
          (Like a kid caught doing something)
          Uh --
                    (Shrugs happily)
          ¡Yo no se! (Yo no say)

                    TIM
          What's it like to be lost and locked in the
          dark for so long?

                    DORA
          It's kinda like going to school in
          Kirkwood.

                    BOB
          Martha said you know a way out!

                    DORA
          ¡Si! (See)

She takes the map from her backpack.

                    MARTHA
          Oh, sure, you don't make him or the crazy
          grunting man scream "backpack" first.

                    DORA
          Let's see . . . We're right here --

                    TIM
          (Looking around)
          We're on a sheet of paper?

Something skitters in the corners. Everyone takes notice, looks
nervous.

                    BOB
          And someone's on it with us!

The Loompa-Loompas emerge from the shadows, giant, oversized
candy bars, lollipops, and other candy props in their hands.
Martha, Dora, Bob, and Tim all shrink to the center of the stage
as the Loompas waddle out, circling tighter and tighter, curious
more than threatening, littering candy wrappers behind them as
they go.

                        MARTHA
You're the ones leaving the candy wrappers
everywhere!

                        BOB
Like they did all over my construction
site . . .  They must be the ones who tore
everything down last night!

                        MARTHA
What do you think they want?

                        TIM
We can ask --

                        BOB
You think we can communicate with them?

                        MARTHA
Such strange little men!

                        TIM
Like elves.

                        DORA
Oh, oh! I know!
          (To the Loompas)
Are you Smurfs?

They stop.

                     BOSS LOOMPA
Do we look blue?

Dora looks at them some more, she picks up a handful of candy
wrappers, and a thought hits her.

                        DORA
Candy, orange faces, funny shoes -- You're
Oompa-Loompas!

                     BOSS LOOMPA
No, we're Loompa-Loompas!

                  MARTHA/DORA/BOB/TIM
Loompa-Loompas?

                        MARTHA
I think you might want to watch the DVD
again --

                    ASSISTANT LOOMPA
From the south of Loompa Land.

                    DORA
What makes you different from Oompa-
loompas?

                BOSS LOOMPA
Oompa Loompas make candy and sell it . . .
We make candy and eat it ourselves!

            ASSISTANT LOOMPA
And leave the wrappers everywhere!

                    TIM
Sounds like a better deal to me.

                    BOB
What are you all doing under Avery?

                BOSS LOOMPA
Our candy factory is down here!

            MARTHA/DORA/BOB/TIM
Candy Factory?

                    TIM
How'd you get a candy factory down here?

            ASSISTANT LOOMPA
It's always been here!

                BOSS LOOMPA
We built the factory back when everything
up there was still a farm.

            ASSISTANT LOOMPA
And then they sold the farm and put the
school playground on top of our factory!

                    BOB
But if you've been here so long, why are
you sneaking out now and tearing down the
new addition to the school I'm trying to
build?

                BOSS LOOMPA
All your construction's collapsing our
tunnels -- and dirt's getting in our
chocolate and ruining it!

Our heroes look to one another as the Loompa-loompas form up for
another dance.

LOOMPA-LOOMPAS

Loompa-Loompa, doompity-dee
someone is messing with our candy!
Loompa-Loompa, doompity-doo
What do you think the orange folk should
do?

END SCENE 4.

END ACT ONE.

ACT TWO

SCENE 1:

The dungeon, right where we last left everyone.

                    BOB
          You can't keep tearing down all the work
          we're doing for the school!

                    BOSS LOOMPA
          We're not tearing anything down! Whatever
          it is you're doing is collapsing our
          tunnels!

An ominous rumble. Dirt and debris sift down from above. Everyone
chokes on the dusty air.

                    ASSISTANT LOOMPA
          And it's ruining our chocolate! What will
          we eat if we can't make candy?

                    DORA
          Fruits and vegetables?

                    ASSISTANT LOOMPA
          As if!

                    BOB
          We're not doing anything to your tunnels!
          Everything we're building is above ground!

                    BOSS LOOMPA
          Well, we're not doing anything to your
          site! We always stay under ground!

                    TIM
          Wait a minute . . .

                    BOB
          Not now.

                    DORA
          I don't think anyone's listening to anyone
          else.

                    MARTHA
          Not now, Aura.

                    DORA
          Dora!

                    TIM
No, she's right. All of you, listen! I've
put up plenty of structures that collapsed.
Bob, your gym addition keeps falling --

                    BOB
I know we're building it solid, so it has
to be whatever these little guys are doing.

                    TIM
And all your tunnels are collapsing --

                    BOSS LOOMPA
We've never had any problems in all the
years we've lived here. Until they started
doing whatever it is they're doing up
there!

                    TIM
Don't you see?

                    MARTHA
I'm afraid not, and I'm both a designer and
a celebrity.

                    TIM
No one's doing anything on purpose here.
There was never a real structure above the
tunnels before, just the trailers and the
playground --

                    BOB
The weight of the new gym's making the
tunnels collapse!

                    BOSS LOOMPA
And the collapsing tunnels are causing your
construction to fall!

                    BOB
I am so sorry! I was blaming you, and it
turns out that the work I'm doing is just
as much to blame.

                    BOSS LOOMPA
But now that we know, we can fix it.

                    BOB
I like the way you think. I promise, I'll
do everything I can to fix all this and
make it right. I'm Bob. And this is Tim,
and Martha, and Dora.

> BOSS LOOMPA
> I'm very pleased to meet you all. And I'm
> sorry we got off on the wrong foot. I'm
> Loompa.

> BOB
> Loompa.

> BOSS LOOMPA
> And this is my assistant Loom-pa.

> BOB
> Loompa.

> ASSISTANT LOOMPA
> No, Loom-pa.

The Loompa-loompas form a line.

> BOB
> Loompa.

> ASSISTANT LOOMPA
> That's pretty close.

> BOSS LOOMPA
> And this is L'oompa, and Loomp-a --

After each Loompah is introduced to Bob, he or she ducks behind the
others and goes to the far end of the line.

> BOSS LOOMPA
> -- Loompah, Loo'mpa, Luumpa, Loomp-uh,
> Miguel, Lou M'pa . . .

> BOB
> There sure are a lot of you!

> BOSS LOOMPA
> -- Oh, yeah -- Lu'umpa, Lume-pah --

MUSICAL NUMBER:

LOOMPA-LOOMPA DANCE

> BOB
> We need to get back through that door, stop
> all the construction before someone down
> here or up there gets hurt!

BOSS LOOMPA

The only way to the surface is through that
door. But you need the key to open it, and
it's been missing since <u>someone</u> threw it
out with the trash the other night.

Assistant Loompa looks around with a guilty "who me?' expression.

MARTHA

The quaint antique gold key I found!

BOSS LOOMPA

You found it? You <u>have</u> it?!?

MARTHA

No . . . I <u>did</u>, but now . . . it's locked
on the other side of the door up there.

BOSS LOOMPA

What kind of boob would leave a key on the
other side of a locked door?

Everyone looks at Tim, except ASSISTANT LOOMPA, who looks at the
ground, the ceiling, etc.

TIM

Hey, who figured out the whole gym-
collapsing-the-tunnels-collapsing-the-gym
thing?

ASSISTANT LOOMPA

That means we have to use the <u>second</u>
key . . .

BOB

Let's go get it!

BOSS LOOMPA

The second golden key is a fairy tale, a
legend. No one knows where it is.

DORA

I do! It's on my map! *¡Mira! (Mee-rah)*
Look! Right here!

BOB

Hey, the map <u>does</u> show another key.

BOSS LOOMPA

The lost second key . . . It's been gone
for years! How do we get to it?

                    DORA
Say it with me: Hallway of Gold Stars,
Tunnel of Cafeteria Mayhem, Teacher's
Lounge Double-Secret Refrigerator!

                    MARTHA
Not again.

Boss Loompa looks at the map

                    BOSS LOOMPA
Oh, we're not going there!

                    TIM
Why not?

                    BOSS LOOMPA
No Loompa-Loompa ever goes to that part of
the tunnels.

                    TIM
But we can't get back without the key!

                    ASSISTANT LOOMPA
And if our tunnels continue collapsing,
we'll have no place to live!

                    BOB
Then we just have to find that key!

                    MARTHA
You mean go down into the tunnels?

                    DORA
We can follow my map!

                    TIM
It looks like the only way we'll get out of
here.

                    BOSS LOOMPA
And save our tunnels!

                    DORA
Then are we ready to go?

                    MARTHA
But what about that 'Roach River?'

                    ASSISTANT LOOMPA
Oh, we sprayed for them ages ago.

                    MARTHA
So no -- ?

She waves her fingers all crazy and buggy in the Loompa's face, the way Dora did to her.

                    ASSISTANT LOOMPA
          No! Now stop it!

                    BOSS LOOMPA
          So you're all going to help us?

                    MARTHA
          Help is such a loaded word, one that sets
          expectations --

                    TIM
                (To Boss Loompa)
          You bet we are

                    ASSISTANT LOOMPA
          It's so good of you!

                    BOB
          When it gets down to it, it's really our
          fault, if no one ever checked to make sure
          the old playground could hold up a new
          building. But we need to get moving!

                    TIM
                (Snapping his helmet light back on)
          Let's go! Dora, you've got the map, so you
          lead.

                    MARTHA
          This all seems very ill-advised. We don't
          have proper clothing, no equipment --
                (Notices Tim)
          -- though we do have a tool --

                    TIM
          Tool Dude.

                    DORA
          Everybody ready?

They all nod and agree. Dora waits an awkward amount of time before replying.

                    DORA (CONT'D)
          Great! ¡Vamos! (Bah-mos) Let's go!

BOSS LOOMPA and ASSISTANT LOOMPA wave and smile broadly, both proud, excited and grateful.

Dora leads the intrepid band on their way into the tunnels. As the last of them exits, ASSISTANT LOOMPA turns to BOSS LOOMPA, both still waving and forcing smiles.

>                    ASSISTANT LOOMPA
> There's <u>no</u> <u>way</u> they're coming back from
> this.

>                    BOSS LOOMPA
> Not a chance.
>           (Smiling wider, waving harder)
> B'bye!

                                        END SCENE 1.


SCENE 2:

Dora sings a too-happy song to herself as she leads the others through the dark passages to the Hallway of Gold Stars. Like most of the rest of the tunnels, it's dark. But here, dozens and dozens of gold stars cover every surface

>                    BOB
> Wow, the kids who go to Avery must be
> really good to earn this many gold stars.

>                    TIM
> Man, those were some tiny people back
> there.

>                    BOB
> They sure were!

>                    TIM
> That one --

>                    BOB
> Loompah?

>                    TIM
> No the other one.

>                    BOB
> Oh, Loompa.

>                    TIM
> Well, the both of 'em, actually. They were
> so short they'd have to climb up on
> something just to get down.

No one reacts to the joke.

>                    TIM (CONT'D)
>         No, really. They're so short, they probably
>         need a stool to pick their own noses.

Everyone but Dora slows as they recognize a low chanting on the air.

>                    BOB
>         Do you all hear that?

Martha and Tim nod while Dora ambles blithely on.

>                    TIM
>         What is it?

>                    MARTHA
>         Whatever it is, it does nothing for the
>         ambiance.

The chanting becomes clearer: voices repeating "Twenty-one, twenty-one, twenty-one . . . " over and over again.

>                    TIM
>         I think it's coming from over here.

Tim follows the sound to a wall with a hole at about eye level. Light shines through the hole.

>                    BOB
>         We don't have time for --

>                    TIM
>         Yeah, I think it's on the other side of
>         this wall.

>                    MARTHA
>         At least whoever it is has adequate
>         lighting back there.

Tim puts his eye to the hole.

>                    TIM
>         Oh, yeah, there's a bunch of those little
>         orange guys on the other side doing all the
>         chanting. Owwww!

Tim jumps back, holding his eye. A finger wiggles through the hole and is then drawn back. The chanting changes to "Twenty-two, twenty-two, twenty-two . . . "

>                    BOB
>         You okay?

>                    TIM
>         Yeah. I can't believe I fell for that one
>         again.

                    DORA
        Look! We're almost at the Tunnel of
        Cafeteria Mayhem!

Dora darts ahead. Everyone else chases after her.

                                        END SCENE 2.


SCENE 3:

The Tunnel of Cafeteria Mayhem. Much like the other tunnels, except
for the rows of doors lining the walls.

                    DORA
        We just head straight down this tunnel, and
        we'll reach the Teachers' lounge and the
        double-secret refrigerator!

Something bangs into one of the doors. They all whirl to look.

                    BOB
        M-maybe someone should check that.

                    TIM
        Nuh-uh.
                (Rubbing his poked eye)
        You know what they say: Fool me once, shame
        on you. Fool me eleven times . . .

He gestures for agreement from the others like "are you with me?"

                    MARTHA
        Eleven times?

The door bumps again.

                    BOB
                (Casual)
        Hey Martha, you're closest. Could you get
        that?

                    MARTHA
        Oh, but of course --

She stops.

                    MARTHA (CONT'D)
        Because opening strange doors has worked
        out _so_ well for me since I came here!

                    DORA
        I'll get it!

Martha jumps back, ready to scream.

Dora flings the door open --

-- Martha jumps into Tim's arms for safety --

-- Bob covers his eyes --

-- There's nothing there.

>                    MARTHA
>          Who's there?

>                    DORA
>          No one.

Martha realizes Tim's still holding her. She looks around,
embarrassed and annoyed. She clears her throat to get him to put her
down.

Tim practically drops her and backs away.

>                    BOB
>          That was weird. Dora, let me see your
>          map . . .

She hands it to him

>                    BOB (CONT'D)
>          Let's see . . . it looks like we've come
>          the right way but - what this say?

>                    DORA
>               (Looks at the map)
>          ¡Guárdese de la momia! (gar-day-say day lah
>          mo-mee-ah) Beware of the mummy!

>                    MARTHA/TIM/DORA
>          Mummy?!?

>                    BOB
>          Are you sure?

>                    DORA
>          Absolutely! ¡Soy bilingue! (soy bee-leen-
>          gway)

Bob's studying the map, turning, trying to get his bearings. While
all eyes are on him, the MUMMY shambles into view, towering behind
Tim. Tim starts shaking his head.

>                    TIM
>          You don't really expect us to believe
>          there's a <u>mummy</u> haunting a grade school in
>          <u>Webster</u> <u>Groves</u>!

He leans back against the Mummy, thinking it's a wall.

> MARTHA
> An Egyptian motif would be so <u>cliché</u> in a
> space like this!

Tim glances over his shoulder, notices the wrappings, starts picking at them absently.

> BOB
> How would a mummy end up here?

Tim happens to look up, into the Mummy's face. He starts hyperventilating and backing away.

> MARTHA
> Perhaps it fell off a truck on its way to a
> museum.

Tim bumps into Dora. She turns, sees the Mummy, and starts making funny scared faces/noises, too.

> BOB
> Y'know, I've dug up a lot of ground, and
> I've never come across anything more scary
> than a broken water
> line --

Dora starts tugging on Martha.

> MARTHA
> Not now, Cora!

> DORA
> M-m-muh --

> MARTHA
> Sorry, "Maura".

Dora keeps tugging on Martha.

> BOB
> -- Let alone a mummy!

> DORA
> M-m-muh --

Martha's had enough and turns to chew out Dora when she sees the Mummy, too.

> MARTHA
> (Strangely composed)
> Eek!

> DORA
> Mummy!

                              BOB
          Mummy?

They all take off running. The Mummy shambles after them.

As "Yakkity Sax" comes up, they all begin ducking in and out of
doors, curtains. At one point, they all chase through a door, Tim
last in line and pausing, unaware Dora's closed the door behind
her -- Tim turns and runs into the shut door.

Eventually, pantomiming, our heroes work together to slam a door on
the Mummy's foot. He hops up and down in pain, then slips and falls.
Dora sits on him while the adults pull off his mask to reveal OLD MAN
AVERY.

                         EVERYONE
          Old Man Avery!

                         MARTHA
          Who's Old Man Avery?

Everyone shrugs.

                         OLD MAN AVERY
          And I would have gotten away with it too,
          if it weren't for you
           meddling --
                    (Does a double-take at the group)
          -- forty-year-olds?

                         MARTHA
          That's it!

She marches off. Everyone else hurries after, annoyed. Dora sticks
her tongue out at Old Man Avery as they exit.

                                        END SCENE 3.


SCENE 4:

At last, they emerge into the Teacher's Lounge, an empty, smoky room
with café tables and chairs and a dark refrigerator.

                         DORA
          Here we are!

                         MARTHA
          We actually made it?

                         BOB
          And that's the refrigerator!

He runs to it, throws open the door --

                         BOB (CONT'D)
          Nothing?

                    TIM
          He's right, it's empty.

                    DORA
     But the map --

                    MARTHA
     The map, the map, the map! I've had it with
     the map!

Bob digs through the fridge.

                    BOB
          It has to be here. The map says so!

Tim takes the map from Dora.

                    TIM
          Say -- the map says it's the Double-Secret
     Refrigerator.

                    BOB
     So?

                    TIM
     So that one's in the middle of the room,
     practically in a spotlight. It doesn't look
     even single-secret.

                    MARTHA
     Another refrigerator!

                    BOB
     Everybody, spread out, look around --

They scatter about the room. Tim's drawn to a book case.

                    TIM
          Like any teacher has time to read books
          during lunch!

He gropes around on it. The book case suddenly swings open so the
audience can't see inside, a brilliant light behind it.

                    TIM (CONT'D)
          Got it!

He disappears beside the door.

                    MARTHA
          Did you find the key?

No answer.

                    BOB
          Tim? What are you doing back there?

>                    (Worried)
>           Are you --

Tim backs into view, slugging back a can of grape soda.

>                BOB (CONT'D)
>           -- getting a drink?

>                     TIM
>           Yeah . . .

>                     BOB
>           Now?!?

>                     TIM
>           We've been hiking around for like, what,
>           hours?

Tim disappears behind the bookcase/door again.

>                TIM (CONT'D)
>           Hey, if you want one, there's still another
>           can of grape and  . . . looks like a peach
>           Nehi! There's also something in Tupperware
>           that should have gone home a long time ago.

He reappears, his expression disgusted, something in his hand about
the size of a schnauzer and just as hairy.

He tosses it aside.

>                TIM (CONT'D)
>           Hang on, there's something else --

He pulls out a large chalice.

>                    DORA
>           That's not a key!

>                   MARTHA
>           Is the key in it?

>                     TIM
>           I dunno . . . there's some kinda liquid in
>           it.

Bob takes the cup from him, squints at it.

>                     BOB
>           There's writing on the side: "Drink deep to
>           find the key --"

>                     TIM
>           I just had a grape soda, so it's all yours,
>           Bob.

The others back away, agreeing.

                    BOB
          Wait, there's more: "Drink only from this
          side of the cup, never from the other side
          of the cup."

                    TIM
               (Points to the cup edge closest to Bob)
          Drink only from this side of the cup --
               (Points to the cup edge
                farthest from Bob)
          -- never from that side of the cup?

                    BOB
               (Pointing)
          Yep, it says to only drink from this side,
          and never from the other side.
               (Holds the cup up to his lips, pauses)
          I wonder why?

                    TIM
          Oh, that's easy.

Tim pushes the far edge of the cup to Bob's mouth, so the near edge
almost touches his chin, the contents dumping all down the front of
Bob's shirt.

                    TIM (CONT'D)
          See?

Martha notices the key tumble from the chalice when it's poured out.

                    MARTHA
          The key!

She picks it up.

                    DORA
          Yay!

                    BOB
          Great work guys!

There's another menacing rumble.

                    BOB (CONT'D)
          Now let's get back fast, and get everything
          fixed!

They start to exit, Dora the last in line.

With a burst of his signature dramatic music, THE PHANTOM OF THE
OPERA steps from the shadows. Our heroes look around for where the
music's coming from, but no one looks in the Phantom's direction.

                    PHANTOM OF THE OPERA
                (With Bela Lugosi hand gestures)
        Sing . . .

Dora seems to be the only one who hears him. She looks toward him,
wide-eyed, hypnotized.

                PHANTOM OF THE OPERA (CONT'D)
                (Again with the hand gestures)
        Sing, my angel of music. Sing!

Dora starts to open her mouth when suddenly Tim pushes past her and
begins belting out "Voices of Spring", (lip-syncing, of course) with
outrageous body language and facial expressions.

The Phantom's taken aback, then shrugs and goes along with it.

                PHANTOM OF THE OPERA (CONT'D)
                (Still with the hand gestures)
        Yes, sing! Mwa-ha-ha --

Seeing the Phantom now, the others look on, extremely confused, as
Tim continues to sing, faces and gestures increasingly outrageous and
silly.

Finally, Martha walks over and simply shoves the Phantom back into
the shadows.

                PHANTOM OF THE OPERA (CONT'D)
        Hey, way - waitaminnit --

He pratfalls into the dark and disappears. Tim shakes his head, the
spell broken.

Bob and Dora look to Martha, questioning.

                    MARTHA
        We're running out of time. (Beat) Besides,
        that was just too silly.

The others all bob their heads in agreement and press on.

                                        END SCENE 4.


SCENE 5:

Our heroes rejoin Boss Loompa and Assistant Loompa near the tiny
magic door.

                    MARTHA
        We have the key!

                ASSISTANT LOOMPA
        No way!

Boss Loompa elbows Assistant Loompa.

                  ASSISTANT LOOMPA (CONT'D)
I mean, <u>great</u> guys!

                  BOSS LOOMPA
Now you can go back to the surface, stop
the construction, and save our candy
factory!

Another ominous rumble.

                  BOB
That rumbling's getting worse. I don't know
if just stopping the project up there's
going to be enough!

                  TIM
What do you mean?

                  BOB
All the tunnels are already damaged from
the weight of the new gym pushing down on
them. Even if we take the weight off, they
may still crack and fall.

                  BOSS LOOMPA
But <u>then</u> what will we do?

                  TIM
I think I know.
        (To the Loompas)
Do you make big chocolate bars?

                  ASSISTANT LOOMPA
You bet!

                  TIM
I mean <u>really</u> big!

                  ASSISTANT LOOMPA
Big enough to reach all the way to the
ceiling big enough for you?

                  TIM
Just about . . . I need the biggest you can
bring, and as many as possible.

                  BOSS LOOMPA
But they're all full of dirt and <u>rocks</u>!

                  TIM
That's what I'm <u>counting</u> on!

                    (To Bob)
          You all go on up. I'll stay here and take
          care of this.

                         MARTHA
          Like when you were "helping" with the gym?
          Or your neighbor's house?

                         TIM
          Deck.

                         BOB
          Tim, I don't know if you should --

                         TIM
          There's no time to talk! I can do this --

Another threatening rumble.

                         TIM (CONT'D)
          You gotta trust me!

Bob starts for the door.

                         BOB
          Let's go! We've got a school and these
          tunnels to save!

He unlocks the door and leads Martha and Dora through.

                                        END SCENE 5.


SCENE 6:

Our heroes -- minus Tim -- enter, blinking at the daylight of the
Avery construction site. Tools are scattered all around. A shouting
crowd of Parents surrounds the still-ruined site and the worried
construction crew.

                    MRS. CRUMBTOPPING
          When do you think you're going to finish?

                    MRS. CLAMCHOWDER
          How are you going to finish?

                    MRS. CAKEMIX
          Yeah! You've wasted the whole summer!

                         MARTHA
                    (To Bob and Dora)
          The whole summer?

                         BUD
          We couldn't finish anything without Bob and
          that designer lady, Martha!

                    CHICO
          And they've been missing for weeks!

                    BOB
          Weeks?!?

                    MARTHA
          How's that possible?

                    MRS. CLAMCHOWDER
          They gym isn't ready and school starts
          tomorrow!

                    DORA
          Maybe time moves differently down in the
          tunnels, the high-energy, high-sugar diets
          of the Loompas fueling a temporal
          distortion that's catapulted us weeks into
          our own future.

Martha and Tim react to Dora's sudden eloquence and expertise.

                    MARTHA
          Or maybe the writer needed a plot device to
          add some urgency to the ending.

                    BUD
          We need Bob and Martha!

                    MRS. CLAMCHOWDER
          Bob and Martha, Bob and Martha, Bob and
          Martha! What's so great about them?

                    BUD
          Well, Bob's a heck of a builder, and he
          knows everything about tools and equipment.

                    CHICO
          And Martha -- she makes things so
          beautiful!

                    CURLEY
          And she's so pretty!

                    MRS. CLAMCHOWDER
          Yeah, but can either of them do this?!?

She explodes with an awkward, crazy gymnastics/dance/martial arts
move. While she heaves, out of breath, everyone backs away
uncertainly.

Bob runs to the center of the excitement. A few of his crew point,
relieved and excited he's back.

                         BOB
          All right everyone, nothing's gone exactly
          as planned, but I know we can turn this
          around and finish --

                    MRS. CRUMBTOPPING
          I still don't like the landscaping!

                    MRS. CLAMCHOWDER
          And the windows -- the windows!

It all devolves into a chaos of shouting and demands and excuses.

                         DORA
                    (To Martha)
          Oh, nobody's listening! The gym will never
          be finished if everybody doesn't stop
          making demands and start working together!

                         MARTHA
          You're right, Sonora!

She marches into the fray.

                         DORA
          Dora!

                         MARTHA
                    (Over her shoulder)
          -- Dora.
                    (Addressing the crowd))
          Excuse me!

She's ignored.

                    MARTHA (CONT'D)
          If I could just have everyone's attention
          for just a moment --

she's shoved aside by the angry crowd, squeezed to the outside of the
group. She huffs at the indignity, and happens to glance at her ankle

Jaw set, Martha looks around, then marches to the edge of the stage,
purposefully sticking her foot with the bracelet over the edge.

The air horn blasts. Everyone but Martha jumps, startled.

                         MARTHA
          Now that we have your attention . . . Tell
          them what you had to say, Cora --

                         DORA
          Dora!

                    MARTHA
-- Dora.

                    DORA
You're all so busy arguing over what you
want for the gym, you've forgotten who it's
really for -- the kids!

Some of the parents consider what she ways; others look ashamed.

                    DORA (CONT'D)
They don't want fancy landscaping or
special windows. They just need a place to
learn, grow, and play! And I bet Mr.
Thebuilder has all that in his plans
already!

                    BOB
I do!

                    BUD
But Bob, something's wrong with the
ground -- Everything we try to put up
collapses!

                    TIM (OS)
I've taken care of that!

Tim enters, lugging something huge behind him.

                MARTHA/BOB/DORA
Tim!

                    TIM
You can get to work! The ground's sturdier
now than it ever was!

                    BOB
How did you fix it?

                    TIM
With a whole lot of these --

He turns over the thing he's carrying to reveal it as a gigantic
Hershey bar!

                    TIM (CONT'D)
 -- Construction-grade chocolate! Strong as
a steel I-beam and a lot more tasty! I
figured with all the sand and dirt and rock
they said was getting into their chocolate,
it would be the perfect thing for bracing!

                    CHICO
School opens tomorrow! There's not enough
time!

                    DORA
If we all work together, we can finish in
no time!

                    BOB
Dora's right! If all the parents here pitch
in, and we work straight through the night,
we can still keep from disappointing all
the kids tomorrow!

                    BUD
But Bob, we don't have any tools!

Tools are scattered everywhere, but no one notices them.

                    BOB
No tools? You had plenty when I left!

                    CHICO
Yeah, but with all the trouble and the
confusion --

                    CURLEY
-- and no one around to make sure we put
everything away every day --

                    CHICO
-- We kinda lost them all.

                    BOB
But if you lost them here, they've got to
be right around somewhere!

                    DORA
I know!
        (Aside)
Can you help us find the tools?
        (Pause)
Great!

                    TIM
Who's she talking to?

                    MARTHA
She's been doing that since I met her!

                    DORA
        (To Bob)
What tools do we need?

> BOB

Well, we need hammers --

> DORA
> (Aside)

Do you see los martillos (lohs mar-tee-yos) -- the hammers?

She waits, staring and blinking, until the kids in the audience start pointing it out. Suddenly, some of the characters on stage notice the hammers and pick them it up.

> DORA
> (Aside)

Great!
> (To Bob)

What else do we need?

> ROB

Uh, saws --

> DORA
> (Aside)

Can you find the saws? ¿Las sierras? (lahs see-air-ahs)

Again, she waits, blinking. Other characters notice the saws suddenly and pick them up.

> DORA
> (Aside)

¡Muy bien! (moo-ee bee-en) You're good at this!

> TIM

I'm gettin' a little creeped out.

> DORA
> (Aside)

How about the <u>rest</u> of the tools? ¿Todos las herramientas? (toe-dose lahs air-ah-me-ent-ahs)

Hopefully, kids in the audience are shouting and pointing, and the characters on stage can just pick anything else up.

Everyone on stage picks up all the tools.

> DORA (CONT'D)
> (Aside)

Great job!
> (To Bob)

Can we get started <u>now</u>?

                    BOB
          You bet we can!

Everyone on stage picks up all the tools as CONSTRUCTION SOUND
EFFECTS come up.

                                        END SCENE 6.


SCENE 7:

Exhausted, everyone stands in front of the new gym. More of Tim's
giant chocolate bars can be seen holding parts of the building up.

Bob, Martha, and Tim size the place up, nodding.

                    BOB
          Wow, that construction grade chocolate
          really comes in handy!

                    MARTHA
          And it lends such a delightful scent to the
          interior spaces!

Dora tugs on Martha's sleeve.

                    DORA
          So, what was your favorite part?

                    MARTHA
          Favorite part? I was terrorized all night
          inside that "school"! We were stalked in
          that horrible dungeon by candy-crazed
          little orange people, had to crawl through
          dark, scary tunnels, got chased by a mummy,
          and then had to build an entire gymnasium
          in under twenty-four hours!

                    DORA
               (Pausing, blinking)
          Mine too!

                    TIM
               (Looking at his watch)
          Your guys done inside yet?

Some of the crew can still be seen inside, working madly with paint
brushes and brooms.

                    BOB
          Should be . . . soon.

Two construction workers bring a long ribbon and some big ceremonial
scissors.

                        BOB
        Good! Bring that around here.

They position the ribbon so it's draped in front of the door.

                        BOB
        That should buy us some time when he shows
        up.

                        TIM
        Who?

DR. SMITH strolls in.

                        BOB
                (Pretending to greet him)
        Dr. Smith!

                        DR. SMITH
        Bob!

                        BOB
        Sorry I've missed you the last few, uh,
        weeks.

                        DR. SMITH
        The gym looks great!

                        BOB
        Thanks.

                        DR. SMITH
        You boys really had me worried when this
        was still a hole in the ground yesterday.

Curley and Bud amble by, a board spanning their shoulders.

                        CURLEY
        We told ya: These things never start to
        take shape until the very end.

                        DR. SMITH
        So I can see.

                        BUD
        Like the genies of the lamp, we are.

Bud stops to pick up a saw. Curley stops and turns to see what he's
doing.

                        CURLEY
        That's not safe!

He nearly smacks an unwitting Dr. Smith with the board. They wander
off.

More parents and construction workers wander on stage, all exhausted, as the workers inside start gathering their stuff.

Dr. Smith notices the big ceremonial scissors in Tim's hand.

> DR. SMITH
> Ah . . . time for the ribbon-cutting?
> Excellent!

He takes the scissors from Tim and approaches the ribbon. Everyone but Dr. Smith starts backing away uncertainly.

> DR. SMITH (CONT'D)
> With the powers vested in me by the Webster
> Groves School District, I hereby declare
> the new Avery Elementary Gym open!

He cuts the ribbon proudly, then looks up just in time to see the façade tip forward and fall straight toward him!

> DR. SMITH (CONT'D)
> (Aside, tiny voice)
> Mommy!

The façade crashes to the ground, somehow managing to fall just so Dr. Smith passes right through an open window.

He stands, shocked, speechless, traumatized. With a few "there-there's", some of the parents help him start shuffling off stage.

Everyone looks accusingly at Tim. He does a "not me" wave of his hands, then starts looking it all over. Martha turns away, crossing her arms, impatient, disappointed. Everyone slowly drifts away.

> BOB
> What do we do now?

Disappointed, he sits down at the front of the stage, back to the gym, and starts gathering up some of his tools and things, humming "I'd Like to Teach the World to Sing."

Behind him, Tim waves over a couple of the Construction guys, and they start helping him pick up the façade.

More people join in the humming.

A few of the Parents join him, then Dora, and then even some of the Loompa-loompas. A few people react, and they all go back to putting the gym back up.

More people join in the humming.

Martha glances them over her shoulder, and then even she, too, uncrosses her arms and goes to help.

At last, the façade is up and secured. The lights come on -- the gym's finally finished!

Bob happens to look up. He does a double take as he sees the school complete. With an enormous grin, he rushes over to join the group, congratulatory.

Arm in arm, everybody sings happily, together.

END SCENE 7.

END ACT TWO.

CURTAIN.

THE END

Steve & Terri's EXCELLENT ADVENTURE

A VERY PLAY

AdVENTURE

# Steve & Terri's Excellent Avery Play Adventure (2009)

*It's the 60th anniversary of the Avery Play, and there's no show!*

*The writer's turned in a script with a story nobody understands. Steve, the Avery Play's director, has been stuck out of town on business. Terri, the show's producer, just came back from vacation. There's no music, no sets, the cast hasn't rehearsed—and the show's tomorrow!*

*When Steve and Terri team up to try to figure out something at the last minute, they wish they could go back in time and bring back the best and funniest characters from past Avery plays. And when Steve discovers the strange power of an odd gift Avery principal Dr. Smith left with him, they get their opportunity and they're off on an adventure through past plays, revisiting favorite characters and stories.*

*But can they get back to 2009 and throw together a show before the first performance?*

I WAS FORTUNATE ENOUGH TO BE IN PLACE AS THE WRITER when the sixtieth anniversary of the Avery Play came up. It was a challenge and a privilege I was eager to take on, but one I was getting stuck solving—How do you tell a story while commemorating the stories that came before? I first thought of the movie *That's Entertainment!* and the amazing job those filmmakers did in telling the MGM story through memorable clips from timeless movies.

It seemed a bit grand for the Avery Play.

I'd also begun thinking along the lines of a "clip show" like they do on TV, where characters reminisce in a framing scene and the rest of the episode is made up of bits of past episodes. It could work, I supposed, but it didn't click for me.

At a get-together with some other Avery parents, someone asked me if I'd come up with an idea for the next Avery Play. I told her not really, and was about to explain the clip show idea and how it wasn't working for me when she said, "Something fun might be like *Back to the Future*, with time travel—"

Right then, the whole story snapped into focus in my mind. But not *Back to the Future*...*Bill & Ted's Excellent Adventure!* A parody of *Bill & Ted* would let me send characters to the past to previous Avery Plays, become part of their story, and even bring characters back to the present for comedy bits where disparate personalities from different shows interact and must work together to save the day.

I set out to do research, borrowing old VHS tapes and scripts from any of the previous actors or directors show might have them stashed in a drawer or box someplace. The initial clip show reminiscences scene ended up as a springboard to get the time travel story started, and then it was a matter of fitting the right characters together to get the story and jokes moving. We worked hard to get the original actors from the past shows wherever we could (the cast for the *Clue* scene was almost entirely the cast from the *Clue*-style comedy-mystery from three years before) and recast when we had to. In the end, we had a great show, one that managed to look to the past while looking forward to the Avery Play's future, recalling memorable bits and performances in a new show that created new memories of its own.

As an anniversary show with numerous in-jokes and references to past shows and performers, this one may be a bit harder for a non-Avery group to put on. But in general, the story's pretty straightforward, the gags broad and the characters and situations well-explained (or explained enough), so an audience shouldn't feel confused or left out of the jokes.

Ready for a discount science fiction epic? A bargain-basement time travel adventure to past Avery Plays? Read on.

"STEVE & TERRI'S EXCELLENT AVERY PLAY ADVENTURE"


Written by

*Patrick Dorsey*

## "STEVE & TERRI'S EXCELLENT AVERY PLAY ADVENTURE"

CHARACTERS:

STEVE, the slightly out-of-it director who's been out of town.

TERRI, the tightly-wound producer who's been on vacation.

TEACHERS, elementary educators anxious for big laughs in a breakout role.

DR. DOE, a school district superintendent.

HONEY, Steve's put-upon and patient wife.

DORA, the plucky bilingual explorer girl who was a hit in last year's show.

MARTHA, a celebrity designer.

MS.PITCH, a stuffy teacher.

ANNIE, loud and untalented but determined to become a star.

ED, a genius in need of an orthodontist.

An ANNOUNCER to tell everyone about out sponsor's products.

STUDENTS who need new shoes.

THE KING, benevolent ruler of Hamelot.

SIR DINTYMOORE, SIR SPAM, SIR CORNEDBEEFHASH, and the rest of the king's dizzy KNIGHTS.

MAGENTA, a domestic.

JEEVES, a handyman.

MISS SCARLET, a suspect.

MRS. PEACOCK, another suspect.

COLONEL MUSTARD, yet another suspect.

MS. WHITE, still another suspect.

PROFESSOR PLUMBER, one more suspect.

INSPECTOR CLOUSTEAU, a clumsy criminologist.

NURSE BOMPART, a nurse.

a CAVEMAN, with no insurance problems.

a FRIEND, who can sympathize.

PETER PAN, peanut butter spokesboy who won't grow up.

THE CAT IN THE HAT, who should not be here while your mother is out.

THE LUNCH LADY, dishing out government-approved "nutrition"

HARRY POTTER, he's all the rage.

CAPTAIN HOOK, with all the punchlines.

LOOMPA-LOOMPAS, like Oompa-Loompas, only different.

JIMBO, a neighbor.

SHAGGY, a hungry hippie ghost chaser.

THE MUMMY, linen-wrapped for freshness (and because *Yakkity Sax* always gets a laugh).

MRS. CLAMCHOWDER, a parent.

INDIANA JONES, from a future Avery Play.

JACK SPARROW, also from a future Avery Play.

THE FRANKENSTEIN MONSTERS, it's pronounced *"Frahn-ken-shteen."*

CLAUDIA, because she can really sing.

DR.SMITH, a school principal.

<u>"STEVE & TERRI'S EXCELLENT AVERY PLAY ADVENTURE"</u>

ACT ONE


SCENE 1:

Open in Steve's living room as an Avery Play meeting is breaking up. TERRI's on the floor with a pile of papers. STEVE is walking a group of TEACHERS to the door, obviously trying to be polite but hurrying them.

                    TEACHER 3
          You have a lovely house! Thanks for having
          us over for the Avery Play meeting!

                    TEACHER 1
          So, remember, my part <u>has</u> to be funny!

                    TEACHER 2
          Mine, <u>too</u>! I want all my kiddos to laugh
          and laugh when they see the play tomorrow
          night!

                    TEACHER 3
          Yeah, but not a lot of lines! I hate
          <u>memorizing</u> things!

                    TEACHER 2
          It's so <u>hard</u>!

                    TEACHER 3
          Can I wear these?

She produces a gigantic pair of prop sunglasses.

                    TEACHER 3 (CONT'D)
          They're <u>hilarious</u>!

                    TEACHER 1
          Slays 'em <u>every</u> time!

                    TEACHER 2
          Ooh, I have a funny wig!

                    TEACHER 1
          And you'll make sure we each get something
          funny to say!

                    TEACHER 3
           -- And not a lot to memorize!

> STEVE
> Sure, sure. Just be there half an hour
> before the show tomorrow night.

> TEACHERS
> (Together)
> Okay!

> STEVE
> Bye, ladies!

Teacher 3 turns, bumps her head on the door, and falls to the floor, knocked out.

The other Teachers hover, unsure.

> TEACHER 2
> What do we do?

> TEACHER 1
> Oh, my! Call someone!

> STEVE
> (Confident, "I got this"-attitude)
> Honeeeeey!

> TEACHER 2
> No, we need a doctor!
> (Aside)
> Is there a doctor in the house?

Out in the audience, DR. DOE stands up.

> DR. DOE
> (Heroic)
> I'm a doctor!

> TEACHER 1, 2 & 3
> (Together)
> Dr. Doe!

He rushes through the audience and springs confidently on stage.

He kneels down over the injured teacher. He takes the teacher's pulse, puts an ear to the teacher's chest.

> TEACHER 3
> Is everything OK?

> DR. DOE
> I don't know . . . I'm not that kind of a
> doctor . . .

Rimshot.

                    DR. DOE (CONT'D)
              (Aside)
      Thank you, I'll be here through May!

Teacher 3 sits up

                    TEACHER 3
      See? I want a funny line like that!

Steve ushers them all out. Dr. Doe lingers.

                    DR. DOE
      Steve, Terri, I'm really looking forward to
      this show. The sixtieth anniversary Avery
      Play! It's a big, big deal, and I'm
      trusting you two are making it special!

                    STEVE
      Nothing to worry about. We're not gonna
      mess this up!

Dr. Doe leaves. Steve closes the door behind him and sags against it.

                    STEVE (CONT'D)
      We are so gonna mess this up!

Terri races over to him and starts poking him with both hands.

                    TERRI
      Focus! There's no time for whining! We have
      to put a whole show together in one night!
      I can't believe you didn't get anything
      done while I was on vacation!

                    STEVE
      I had to go out of town for work. Like, a
      bunch of times. Hey, you were gone too!

                    TERRI
      And Tahiti was very nice, thank you for
      asking! (sighs) Nobody thought to ask about
      rehearsals?

                    STEVE
      You know how everyone is about showing up
      for rehearsals . . .

                    STEVE & TERRI
              (Together)
      Yeah . . .

>                    TERRI
>
> Okay, the play's tomorrow night! I've seen
> the emails -- at least we've got a finished
> script, right?

>                    STEVE
>
> Sort of.

>                    TERRI
>
> What do you mean, sort of? Did Pat write
> one or not?

>                    STEVE
>
> He did, but --

>                    TERRI
>
> But what?

>                    STEVE
>
> Read it! It's like a dictionary of old
> radio and vaudeville jokes! I mean, look at
> this one . . .

>                    TERRI
>
> "Niagara Falls!?!"

>                    STEVE
>
> "Slowly I turned, step by step, inch by
> inch" -- What does that even mean?

>                    TERRI
>
> Well, we have to do something. We need to
> get organized --

>                    STEVE
>
> I got started on that before you came over.

>                    TERRI
>
> Great!

>                    STEVE
>
> Everything's sorted into two folders --

He pulls out a slim folder with two pages in it.

>                    STEVE
>
> Director jobs --

He tucks it under his arm, then pulls out a big archive file box
crammed with papers and drops it in Terri's lap.

>                    STEVE
>
>    -- And producer jobs.

Terri slumps as she starts going through the box. Steve opens his file, takes out the two sheets of paper in it, and starts looking them over.

> TERRI
> Acquire a script, organize ticket
> sales . . . arrange for costumes and sets!
> Steve, you didn't even --

> STEVE
> I believe that all falls under <u>producer</u>
> <u>jobs</u>.

> TERRI
> I believe I want to fall under a bus . . .

They continue going over their papers. Steve looks confused at one of his two sheets and tries to hand it to Terri.

> STEVE
> Oops . . . I believe this falls under
> producer jobs.

> TERRI
> I believe you're about to fall down a
> flight of stairs.

> STEVE
> I could probably just add it to my
> stack . . .

Steve flops on the couch

> TERRI
> What are you doing?

> STEVE
> I always do my best thinking in front of
> the TV.

He pulls out a giant, futuristic TV REMOTE all silvery and laser-sticker shiny and covered in blinking lights.

> TERRI
> Guess you don't have much trouble losing
> that between the sofa cushions.

> STEVE
> Dr. Smith gave this to me.

> TERRI
> What did you do to him?

STEVE
No, he stopped by earlier. Must've been
headed to a costume party --

TERRI
In March.

STEVE
I dunno, his suit was all -- and his
hair -- wearing a tie that was . . .
Anyway, he gave me this and told me it
might come in handy. Then he gave me a big
bag of videotapes of . . . of old Avery
plays! That's it!

TERRI
What?

STEVE
We'll watch these tapes for ideas! Maybe we
can just put together a show of highlights
from other shows! They do that all the time
on TV when they run out of ideas!

TERRI
Hey, that's pretty good thinking! I don't
know why everyone says you're such a boob!

STEVE
Well, sure, I mean, I can come up with --
Hey, who says I'm a boob?

Terri takes a tape from the bag.

TERRI
All right, here's last year's.

STEVE
Good. We'll have an easy time finding
people from last year's show.

Terri puts the tape in the VCR. Steve points the giant remote, but
nothing happens. He pounds the button a few more times.

STEVE
Honeeeeey! The new remote's not working!

HONEY (OS)
It probably needs new batteries. You should
change them!

Steve makes a "yeah, right" face and shakes the remote before
pointing it again. The TV comes on.

                    STEVE
        Nevermind, I got it.
              (Beat)
        Honeeeeey? Could you bring Terri and me a
        couple drinks and some snacks? We've got a
        lot of work ahead of us to get ready for
        the show tomorrow night, and we're right in
        the middle of --

                    HONEY (OS)
        Sure thing, Pookie.

                    TERRI
        Pookie?!?

                    STEVE
        Sure, it's Latin, the masculine form
        of . . . I mean, y'know, a recognition of
        strength and . . . Ahh, she loves *Garfield*
        and started calling me that back when we
        were dating.

                    TERRI
              (Giggling)
        Pookie --

                    STEVE
        Cut it out!

                    TERRI
        Poo-ookie!

Steve bonks her on the head with the remote.

                    TERRI (CONT'D)
        Oww!

They start slapfighting (silly) then wrestle for the remote.

HONEY enters in an apron and pearls, carrying a tray with drinks and
bowl of popcorn.

                    HONEY
        Here you go, root beer and -- What's going
        on in here?

As they wrestle for the remote, it gets pointed at Honey and makes a
strange sound.

Honey suddenly walks backwards --

                    HONEY (CONT'D)
        ?ereh ni no gniog s'tahW -- dna reeb toor
        ,og uoy ereH

-- and exits.

Steve and Terri stop fighting.

> STEVE
> What just happened?

> TERRI
> Your wife just walked in and then walked
> out all backwards, like --

> STEVE
> Like she was rewinding.

> TERRI
> How --

Steve pushes a button on the remote.

Honey enters, with a tray with drinks and bowl of popcorn.

> HONEY
> Here you go, root beer and --

Steve hits the remote again. Honey suddenly walks backwards --

> HONEY (CONT'D)
> -- dna reeb toor ,og uoy ereH

 -- and exits.

> TERRI
> Okay, that's freaky.

> STEVE
> Yeah it's freaky . . . and awesome!

> TERRI
> How does it do that?

> STEVE
> Look! It's got a TV - Satellite - Reality
> switch! We must've pushed it into the
> reality mode when we were wrestling over
> it.

Terri jumps off the sofa.

> TERRI
> That's just weird, Steve.

> STEVE
> The rewind works. I wonder if --

He hits a button. Honey races out as she did before only much, much
faster and sets down the tray.

                    HONEY
          HereyougorootbeerandpopcornIhope
          youtwodon'thavetoworkkallthrough
          thenightonhis.

Terri is also racing around, packing up the box of producer papers.

                    STEVE
          Whoa --

He hits a button. Honey picks up the tray and races out backwards.

                    HONEY
          .sihnothginehthguorhtllakrowot
          evaht'nodowtuoyepohInrocpopdna
          reebtooroguoyereH

Terri races backwards and puts down everything she picked up, then sits back on the couch.

                    TERRI
          What just happened?

                    STEVE
                (Inspecting the remote with awe)
          The remote must only affect things that
          aren't on the couch with it.

                    TERRI
          Do you know what this means?

                    STEVE
          Yes! I can rule the world and never get off
          my couch! *Mwa-ha-ha* --

Terri pokes him over and over with both hands.

                    TERRI
          Focus!

                    STEVE
          Ow . . .

                    TERRI
          It means we don't have to just copy scenes
          from the earlier Avery plays -- we can go
          back in time and get all the funniest
          characters from the past plays, bring them
          back to now and put them in tomorrow
          night's play! They'll be rehearsed,
          fresh --

                    STEVE
          They'll know all their lines!

> TERRI
> As well as they ever do! We won't even need
> a script! It'll <u>work</u>!

> STEVE
> Where do we start?

> TERRI
> Last year, with the character that made
> <u>everyone</u> laugh!

They get down on the couch like it's a bobsled. Steve holds up the remote, pushes the button, and in a flash of special light and sound effects, the couch shoots off into time.

END SCENE 1.


SCENE 2:

Backstage at "Lost at Avery." Steve's sofa slides into view in a burst of light and sound.

> STEVE
> We made it!

> TERRI
> We're really in the past!

> STEVE
> Yep, last year's play.

Applause and laughs sound, distant.

> TERRI
> (Pointing, a little freaked out)
> So, out there, on stage, it's --

> STEVE
> It's 2008, and the Friday night performance
> of "Lost at Avery." Wow, look at these
> sets! You can see what a great construction
> job we did last Spring --

> TERRI
> (Poking)
> Focus!

> STEVE
> Who are we here to get?

> TERRI
> I thought that was pretty obvious. We're
> gonna need laughs in our new show, so I
> thought for sure we could use --

DORA pops out.

> DORA
> ¡Hola!

Steve screams.

Dora screams.

Steve starts to scream again, but Terri clamps a hand over his mouth.

> TERRI
> Knock it off! We have to be quiet!

> STEVE
> Right. Because we might disrupt that
> timestream with our presence --

Terri glares at him.

> STEVE (CONT'D)
> (Sheepish)
> -- they said that in a time-travel TV show
> I watched once --

> TERRI
> That and we already did that incongruous-
> science-talk gag in last year's show.

> DORA
> Hi! I'm Dora! Dora the --

> TERRI
> We know, we know. Listen, Dora, we need you
> to come with us for a minute or two.

> DORA
> I'd love to help --

> TERRI
> Great!

She takes Dora's hand and starts to lead her off. But Dora doesn't
budge.

> DORA
> -- But I'm in the play, and I don't want
> to miss my cue!

> STEVE
> Oh, sure, now you're worried about your
> cues!

                    DORA
You made a big deal about it in rehearsal!
Except I thought you were on stage in this
scene.

                    STEVE
            (Aside to Terri)
That's right! I was the director last year,
too!

                    TERRI
She can't tell you're not this year's
Steve!

                    DORA
*Ay yi yi,* you look so much <u>older</u> than last
night! And have you lost some <u>hair</u>?

                    TERRI
Apparently she <u>can</u> tell --

                    STEVE
I got an idea!
            (To Dora)
It's just the light backstage here. Makes
everyone look less attractive.

                    DORA
Then you should try stay out of this light!

                    STEVE
I'll do that --

                    DORA
I mean try <u>really</u> hard --

                    STEVE
Right --

                    DORA
 -- Like never go anywhere <u>near</u> this kind
of light. Ever.

                    STEVE
            (To Terri)
It's only been a year! A rough year, sure,
but I didn't think I looked --

Terri elbows him.

                    STEVE (CONT'D)
So, uh, Dora, did you get the, uh, last
script revisions?

                    TERRI
                 (To Steve)
         Good!

                    DORA
         Script revisions?

                    STEVE
         Uh, yeah, we've had to re-block this whole
         scene.

                    DORA
         In the middle of the play?

                    STEVE
         That's live theatre for ya!

                    DORA
         Oh no! I need my script!
                 (Aside)
         Can you help me find my script?

Steve falls right into the game --

                    STEVE
         Sure!

 -- Terri, on the other hand . . .

                    TERRI
         You've gotta be flippin' <u>kidding</u> me!

Dora waits and waits while Terri's migraine gets worse.

                    DORA
                 (Finally)
         Great!
                 (Aside)
         Do you see my copy of the script anywhere
         backstage?
                 (Beat)
         That's right! I <u>did</u> leave it in the
         dressing room!

                    STEVE
         How do we get to the dressing room from
         here, Dora?

                    DORA
         We'll use the map!

Terri can't take much more of this.

                    DORA (CONT'D)
         Say "Backpack!"

> STEVE

Back --

> TERRI
> (Forcing a smile)

Y'know, I think I saw a copy of the script on the sofa over there.

> DORA

But *no es mio (no ess me-oh)* -- it's not mine! And that would be taking something that belongs to someone else!

> TERRI

I'm pretty sure it's a copy for everybody to use.

> DORA

Really?

> TERRI

Sure. It was stamped "Copy for Everyone to Use." Take a look --

Terri follows Dora to the sofa.

> TERRI (CONT'D)

-- I think it's stuck between the cushions.

> STEVE

Nah, that's probably my TV Guide --

Terri whirls on him. Steve does a startle take and gets it suddenly.

When Dora leans over the sofa, Terri shoves her. Dora's legs kick manically as Steve and Teri jump on the sofa.

> TERRI

Where to now?

> STEVE

Back another year, for some more characters everyone will remember!

> TERRI

Y'know, Steve, I have to admit I wasn't completely sure about this idea to start, but now I am.

> STEVE

Well, okay, maybe we can try something else, then --

                    TERRI
     No, I'm sure it's going to <u>work</u>! The 2009
     Avery Play's future's looking bright.

                    STEVE
     So bright, we gotta wear shades!

Steve hits the remote, and in a flash, they're off.


MUSICAL NUMBER:

A dance performance to "My Future's So Bright, I Gotta Wear Shades"


MARTHA put-together in a blonde wig, celebrity jewelry, and giant,
glowing, house-arrest anklet, backs through the curtain from
"onstage."

                    MARTHA
                (Calling out of the side of her mouth)
     Flora! Flora, you're on!
                (Beat)
     We need you and your map to go look for the
     gold key!
                (Beat)
     So we can get out of this dun-geon!
                (Beat)
     Auro-<u>ra</u>!
                (Looks over her shoulder, sees no one)
     Oh, <u>poo</u>!

                                        END SCENE 2.

SCENE 3:

Uptight teacher MS. PITCH, with a clipboard in hand, and a STUDENT
are on stage for "Grade School Reunion Musical." Ms. Pitch is nodding
approvingly.

                    MS. PITCH
     Thank you, that was a lovely audition.

The student walks off as Ms. Pitch looks at her clipboard.

                    MS. PITCH (CONT'D)
     Annie? You're up!

ANNIE walks out in a red dress and insane ORANGE FRIGHT WIG.

ANNIE
(Shouting)
THANK YOU, MS. PITCH!

One after the other, down to up, Steve, Terri, and Dora suddenly poke their heads out from behind the curtain.

STEVE
Here we are. 2007 and "Grade School Reunion Musical."

DORA
So you want to bring someone back from this play, too?

STEVE
And a whole <u>bunch</u> more from other Avery plays.

TERRI
Shh! Here we go!

MS.PITCH
Uh, yes. So, what will you be performing for your audition?

ANNIE
I'M GOING TO SING!

MS. PITCH
Annie, dear, why are you shouting?

ANNIE
I'M NOT SHOUTING, MS. PITCH. I'M <u>PROJECTING</u> --

MS. PITCH
Oh, I see --

ANNIE
 -- PLAYING TO THE CHEAP SEATS!!

MS. PITCH
Oh, of course. Um, you know, Annie, this isn't a very big auditorium, so you may not have to, ah, <u>project</u> so much.

ANNIE
BUT WILL THEY BE ABLE TO HEAR ME IN THE BACK?

MS. PITCH

I'm sure they'll be able to hear you in
Kirkwood, dear. So let's try it a little
softer.

ANNIE

OKAY!

MS. PITCH

Now, Annie, whenever you're ready.

ANNIE

(Shouting loud and hitting every note
but the right ones)
THE SUN WILL COME DOWN, TOMORROW --

Steve, Terri, and Dora's faces contort in agony, everything from
plain pain to getting-ready-to puke expressions.

STEVE

Maybe this one isn't a good choice.

TERRI

Are you kidding? Listen to the crowd --
this is gold!

ANNIE

-- BET YOUR BOTTOM DOLLAR THAT
TOMORROW THERE'LL BE HUNS --

MS. PITCH

Annie, Annie, uh, thank you. That was
very . . . forceful. But I don't think you
have the lyrics right.

ANNIE

ARE YOU SURE?

DORA

I am!

Terri covers Dora's mouth. The three of them disappear again behind
the curtain.

MS. PITCH

Yes, I'm afraid so. It's "The sun will come
out tomorrow" -- not down. It's a happy
song. And there's no Huns.

ANNIE

OH. THAT WOULD BE DIFFERENT!

                    MS. PITCH

Yes . . . so why don't you go look up the lyrics, practice it some more, and you can try out for the <u>next</u> musical when we have one.

                    ANNIE

OKAY. THANK YOU MS. PITCH.

                    MS. PITCH

Thank you, Annie. But go get that practice in now! Someplace far, <u>far</u> away . . .
        (To the other GSRM characters)
Now, everyone, we'll take a ten minute break  . . .

Ms. Pitch and the other GSRM characters wander offstage, leaving Annie alone.

Steve and Terri enter and approach her.

                    TERRI

Hi, Annie.

                    ANNIE

HI, TERRI! HOW'S THE BASKETBALL DANCE GOING?

                    TERRI
        (To Steve)
That's <u>right</u>, I <u>did</u> help choreograph the basketball team dance for that show.
        (To Annie)
Actually, that's what I wanted to talk to you about. I need some more dancers.

                    ANNIE

OH, GOOD! I DIDN'T GET TO SHOW MS. PITCH MY DANCING!

Steve and Terri start to lead her away.

                    TERRI

Great! If you can just follow me, I'll take you to the rehearsal --

                    ANNIE

I DANCE <u>ALMOST</u> AS WELL AS I <u>SING</u>!

Steve and Terri stop short and do a double-take. Steve clutches at his chest in bug-eyed horror.

                         TERRI
                    (Forcing a smile)
           Can't . . . wait . . .

They start off again, Annie in tow. As they reach the sofa, Dora pops
out again.

                         DORA
           ¡Hola!

Steve screams.

Dora screams.

Annie screams.

                         TERRI
           Stop with the popping out and shouting
           ¡Hola! already!

                         DORA
           I found someone else for the play!

Steve and Terri and Annie all look around, confused.

                         STEVE
           Who?

Dora reaches behind the curtain and pulls out ED, in full nerd outfit
and AWFUL TEETH.

He points at them with both fingers, doing the little pistol thing.

                         ED
                    (Trying to sound cool)
           Ed.

Steve and Terri look at each other, like they're not going to do it.

Dora stares wide-eyed and nodding, like she's trying to convince them
to buy her a puppy, while Ed keeps up the pointing/shooting thing,
like he thinks it makes him seem cool.

                         TERRI
           Ahh, bag 'im and let's go.

                         ANNIE
           DID YOU FIND HIM ON YOUR MAP?

                         DORA
           No, I was exploring backstage and tripped
           over him!

Dora darts ahead and jumps on the sofa. Then everyone else piles on.

                         DORA
           Are we going back to the future?

                         STEVE
          I thought we were doing the "Bill & Ted"
          thing --

                         TERRI
               (Poking Steve)
          Focus!
               (To Dora)
          We still have room on the sofa and need
          more characters. So we're going back to
          another Avery Play.

Steve raises the remote.

                         STEVE
          Everybody ready?

He pushes the Rewind button, and with a flash of lights and sounds,
they take off.


                                                 END SCENE 3.


SCENE 4:

Everything's black. The sofa's center stage. Lights start flashing
crazily. Everyone but Dora and Ed seem worried.

                         TERRI
          Steve, stop rewinding now! We don't want to
          go so far back in time that Avery isn't
          even built yet!

                         STEVE
          I can't stop it!

                         TERRI
          What do you mean?!?

                         STEVE
          The remote's stuck or something! I keep
          hitting the buttons but it won't stop or
          pause or fast-forward or anything!

                         DORA & ANNIE
               (Together)
          Oh no!!

                         TERRI
          What happens if we don't stop?

                        STEVE
          I don't know! We could end up rewinding all
          the way to the beginning of time!

                        DORA
          What will we find there?

                        ED
          A primordial hot and dense initial
          singularity that signals the breakdown of
          general relativity!

                        STEVE
                  (To Terri)
          Why didn't you poke him for saying all
          that?

                        TERRI
          He's the science nerd! That's his job in
          the story!

Steve starts shaking and banging the remote. There's a flash,
everyone cries out, and the lights wink out.

                                        END SCENE 4.


COMMERCIAL

                        ANNOUNCER
          Steve and Terri's Excellent Avery Play
          Adventure will be right back after this
          message.

Two STUDENTS jog out in front of the curtain wearing big smiles and
brand-new shoes. They mime how happy they are, and how they agree
with all the great things the announcer says.

                        ANNOUNCER (CONT'D)
          New Scholastic Shoes! The shoes that make
          you smarter just by slipping them on! Tired
          of falling grades? Missing all the complex
          plays in your favorite team sports? Not any
          more with new Scholastic Shoes! The only
          shoes scientifically shown to raise your IQ
          by 25% or your money back! Available in
          athletic, loafer, and hiking boot styles.
                  (Beat)
          Common side effects of Scholastic Shoes
          include:

The two students look a little concerned.

> ANNOUNCER (CONT'D)
> Abdominal pain, anxiety, constipation,
> difficulty swallowing, dizziness, dry
> mouth, fatigue, excessive gas, headache,
> decreased appetite, sweating, indigestion,
> insomnia, nausea, nervousness, rash, pain,
> sleepiness, sore throat, tingling, and
> vomiting.

The two students look at their shoes, worried, and react with shock
and dismay at the worst of what the Announcer lists.

> ANNOUNCER (CONT'D)
> Less common side effects may include:
> Abnormal dreams or thoughts, acne,
> bruising, cold, clammy skin, pinkeye,
> coughing, exaggerated feeling of well-
> being, fainting, feeling faint upon arising
> from a sitting or lying position, blushing,
> hair loss, hallucinations, hemorrhoids,
> hiccups, hot flashes, inability to stay
> seated, increased salivation, itching, lack
> of coordination, leg cramps, memory loss,
> movement problems, muscle weakness, need to
> urinate during the night, nosebleeds,
> purplish spots, paranoia, ranting, rapid
> mood shifts, sleepwalking, swollen wrists
> and ankles, temporary blindness, tooth
> grinding, throbbing, twitching, and
> yawning.

They try desperately to yank their shoes off.

> ANNOUNCER (CONT'D)
> Women who are nursing, pregnant or could
> become pregnant should not wear or handle
> Scholastic Shoes.
> > (Beat)
> Do not inhale any fumes from Scholastic
> shoes. Discard Scholastic Shoes immediately
> should they become worn, cracked, or begin
> leaking fluid. Rinse eyes or skin
> immediately and induce vomiting after
> contact with leaked fluids. Do not stare
> directly at interior of Scholastic Shoes.

They switch to very carefully, gently nudging their shoes off.

> ANNOUNCER (CONT'D)
Scholastic shoes cannot be shipped to
Delaware, Hawaii, or the Netherlands.
>> (Beat)
Scholastic Shoes! Get yours today!

END COMMERCIAL.

SCENE 5:

The lights come on slowly. The sofa's in the middle of a field, with everyone sprawled over it.

> TERRI
Let me see that remote!

She fiddles with it.

> TERRI (CONT'D)
Look! The little light's not going on when you push the buttons! The batteries must be dead!

> STEVE
Oh! And I told my wife to change those!

> DORA
Do you know where we are?

> ED
How about when we are?

> STEVE
No.

> TERRI
No idea.

> DORA
>> (Pointing in the distance)
Maybe we can ask at that castle!

> EVERYONE
Castle?!?

> DORA
And maybe they'll have some batteries!

> STEVE
They won't have any batteries! Batteries probably won't be invented for like a thousand years!

                    TERRI
          Just calm down. Just because it's a castle
          doesn't mean we're way back in ancient
          times or anything.

                    STEVE
          Yeah, but that castle looks <u>new</u>! And all
          the castles I've ever seen pictures looked
          really, <u>really</u> old!

                    DORA
          We can ask those guys.

                    TERRI
          Which guys?

                    DORA
          The ones in armor riding this way.

                    STEVE
          Hang on -- We don't have the budget for
          horses and guys in armor!

                    TERRI
                (Poking)
          <u>Focus</u>! Quick! Annie, Ed, Dora -- hide!
          Behind the sofa!

                    ANNIE
          WHAT FOR?

                    TERRI
          And <u>stay</u> <u>quiet</u>! In case something happens,
          one of our groups might be able to help the
          other.

Annie, Ed, and Dora duck behind the sofa.

                    KING (OS)
          Dis-mount!

The very-important KING, SIR DINTYMOORE -- with a big droopy
moustache that hangs over his mouth and puffs out whenever he
talks -- and several KNIGHTS including SIR SPAM and
SIR CORNEDBEEFHASH gallop in on HOBBY HORSES.

                    STEVE
          Cool! I was wondering how we'd handle the
          horses-on-stage thing!

Terri smiles wide, trying to seem harmless and friendly. She does an
awkward curtsy.

                    TERRI
        Uh, hello, your, er, highness?

                    KING
        What ho! I am King Gluteus!

                    STEVE
                (Trying not to laugh)
        Gluteus <u>Maximus</u>?

                    KING
        Indeed! Yea, it is good ye know of me,
        especially since you've dumped your
        furniture in my potato field!

                    TERRI
        And we'll get it moved for you immediately,
        if you have any . . . batteries?

                    KING
        I know not of this word "batteries" -- do
        you, knights?

The knights all shrug.

                    STEVE
                (To Terri)
        I told you we were in the Dark Ages or
        something!

                    TERRI
                (To Steve)
        Maybe we can figure something out.
                (To King)
        Do you have a wizard we could talk to? Or
        your alchemist?

The king's shaking his head like he doesn't understand.

                    STEVE
        Like a royal . . . smart person?

Terri rolls her eyes. But the King's face lights up.

                    KING
        Ah, yes, the Royal Smart Person!

Steve sticks his tongue out at Terri.

                    KING (CONT'D)
        Ye shall have to return with us to yon
        castle to meet him.

                    TERRI
        If it wouldn't be a bother . . .

The King starts to circle the sofa. Though the King doesn't see them yet, Steve notices Annie's bright orange hair jutting over the back of the sofa. He throws himself across the sofa to block the King's view.

The King looks suspicious.

> KING
>
> Pray, tell, what hidest thou behind yon cushiony bench?

> STEVE
>
> Behind . . . Oh, behind this cushiony bench? Nothing.

> KING
>
> Nothing.

> STEVE
>
> Nope, nothing. Not a thing. Not one single thing at <u>all</u>.

> KING
>
> Then what did I spy back there, all curly and orange?

> STEVE
>
> Oh, just the . . . curly . . . orange, uh, . . . <u>thing</u> I put back there.

Terri throws her arms up in disgust.

> KING
>
> Ah, very well, then! Come! To the castle!

Terri does a double-take, astonished that he bought <u>that</u>.

> TERRI
>
> So, your majesty, what - what castle is that, anyway?

> KING
>
> Yon castle is mine home: Hamelot!

> SIR DINTYMOORE
>
> Hamelot!

> SIR SPAM
>
> Hamelot!

> SIR CORNEDBEEFHASH
>
> Hamelot!

MUSICAL NUMBER:

A chaotic dance performance to "Knights of the Roundtable" from *Monty Python and the Holy Grail*

                    STEVE
        I don't want to go there! It's too silly!

                    KING
        But before you may speak to the Royal Smart
        Person, you must first perform a task for
        me!

                    STEVE & TERRI
                (Together)
        A task?!?!

                    KING
        Yes. Something less than a "knightly
        quest", more than a "little errand."

                    STEVE
                (Looking at his wrist,
                 which has no watch)
        Wow, it's getting late.

                    TERRI
        You're not even wearing a <u>watch</u>.

                    STEVE
        Yeah, but with all these potatoes around
        here, I bet we could make one of those
        potato clocks, like the Avery kids do for
        the science fair --

Ed pops up from behind the sofa, with a "that's it!" snap of the
fingers --

                    ED
        Eureka!

-- and disappears behind it again.

                    KING
        Our lands have been terrorized by the
        Perilous Squirrel of Perilousness --

                    TERRI
        A squirrel?!?

> KING

-- And so far, my brave knights, Sir Dintymoore, Sir Spam, and Sir Cornedbeefhash, have been unable to overcome it.

> TERRI

A squirrel?!?

> SIR DINTYMOORE

We just started looking for outside help, and here you drop in!

> STEVE
>> (To Terri)

I don't think we've got a choice.

> TERRI
>> (To Steve)

The remote's not working -- We have to do something to try get back to 2009. Besides, it's a squirrel. How hard can it be?
>> (To King)

Where do we find this Perilous Squirrel?

> SIR DINTYMOORE

-- of Perilousness.

> TERRI

Right.

> SIR DINTYMOORE

Take heed: You don't want to face this squirrel when it's enraged.

> TERRI
>> ("Yeah, whatever"-tone)

We'll try to avoid "enraging" it.

> STEVE

Wait . . . how do we avoid doing that?

> SIR SPAM

Don't touch his nuts!

> TERRI

Excuse me?

> STEVE

No problem there.

                    SIR DINTYMOORE
The Perilous Squirrel of Perilousness is
very protective of his nuts.

                    STEVE
Understandable.

                    SIR DINTYMOORE
He hoards them in his lair, in a great huge
pile he guards jealously.

                    TERRI
So how do we find it?

                    SIR CORNEDBEEFHASH
The squirrel dwells in yon hollow tree,
over the hills and off in the dark glade.
The way is long and tortuous and confusing,
with little hope for success.

                    STEVE
Like graduating from Kirkwood.

                    SIR DINTYMOORE
Whoa, whoa, it's not that
bad.

                    STEVE
          (To Terri)
You think Dora has a map to get us there?

                    TERRI
I can see the tree from here. It's not far.
          (Shouting over the sofa
           to the others)
We should be back soon, so don't wander
off.

                    SIR SPAM
We shall remain here.

                    KING
          (Inspecting the sofa)
And perhaps try out yon cushiony bench on
the royal seat.

                    STEVE
          (To Terri)
You think we should ask for any tools
or . . . weapons?

                         TERRI
          It's a <u>squirrel</u>, Steve. All I need's a rake
          and a sack.

The Knights produce these out of nowhere and hand them to Steve and
Terri.

                         TERRI (CONT'D)
          See? They've done this before. Now, come
          on. The sooner we get this done, the sooner
          we see the king's Smart Person and figure a
          way out of this deleted scene from *The
          Cable Guy*.

The King plops himself down on the sofa and smiles comfortably as
Steve and Terri exit.


                                             END SCENE 5.

                                             END ACT ONE.

ACT TWO

SCENE 1:

The knights are on the ground, asleep against the sofa, all snoring in the middle of the potato field. Terri and Steve run screaming and stumbling back onstage. The knights don't wake up or react.

                    TERRI
          Ahh . . . Can you believe how fast that
          squirrel was! And mean!

                    STEVE
          What did you expect? You touched his nuts!

                    TERRI
          By accident! I fell in the big pile of 'em
          when it jumped out!

                    STEVE
          I was going to lure it out of the tree! We
          could've surprised it!

                    TERRI
          It was a bad plan, Steve!

                    STEVE
          But no-ooo! Terri the bigshot producer just
          had to leap in with her mighty rake!

                    TERRI
          He stuck his head out of the tree! I
          thought I had him!

                    STEVE
          At least it was greedy enough to chase
          after the walnuts you threw! I don't know
          how we would've gotten away, otherwise.
                    (Beat)
          They'll never let us meet that Royal Smart
          Person now!

                    TERRI
          We don't even know if he can help us at
          all!

                    STEVE
          We have to tell the King something!

                    TERRI
        We can tell him anything if he bought that
                (Dumb guy voice)
        "Uh, curly, uh, orange . . . duh, thing"
        story you gave him earlier.

                    STEVE
        It worked, didn't it?
                (Sad)
        You don't have to be so mean . . .

The audience -- or our plants in the audience -- go "Awww."

                    TERRI
        Aww, I'm sorry Steve. It's just, after
        coming home from vacation, and then diving
        into getting the Avery Play ready and then
        getting trapped in the Dark Ages eight
        hundred years in the past . . . I'm kinda
        crabby.

                    STEVE
        It's not your fault, Terri.
                (Beat)
        It's Pat's fault! If he'd turned in a
        script we could use --

                    TERRI
        -- We wouldn't have had to go through any
        of this! Just wait 'til we get back to
        2009 . . .

                    STEVE
        But how are we going to do that?

Ed pops out from behind the sofa.

                    ED
        I found a way!

The King and Knights stir. Terri and Steve jump.

                    TERRI
        Shh! Don't wake them up! We don't know what
        we're going to tell them!

                    ED
        Tell 'em we're leaving!

                    STEVE
        How? We don't have any batteries, and they
        won't be invented for like another thousand
        years!

                    ED
          Actually, you gave me the idea, Steve! I
          don't know why everyone says you're such
          a boob!

                    STEVE
          Sure, I can come up with -- Who says I'm
          a boob?!?

                    TERRI
               (Poking Steve)
          Focus!
               (To Ed)
          What did you come up with?

Ed reaches behind the sofa and produces the remote, which is now
attached by a tangle of wires to two oversized BAKING POTATOES!

                    ED
          You mentioned making a potato clock, and I
          saw I could harness the potatoes around us
          to power the remote.

                    STEVE
          And that worked?

                    ED
               (Aside)
          Kids, ask your science teachers!

                    TERRI
          Awesome! We can get out of here and don't
          even need to wake these knights up! Dora,
          Annie, come on!

Dora and Annie climb over the sofa and sit next to Sir Dintymoore.

                    DORA
          What about him?

                    STEVE
          If we wake him up, he might wake up the
          others!

                    TERRI
          Then it looks like he's about to make his
          stage debut -- in 2009! Everybody get your
          fannies on the futon, and let's leave the
          past behind!

They all pile on, jostling the knight. He starts to wake up.

>                    SIR DINTYMOORE
>          Huh -- wha --

Steve points the remote, hits the button with a flourish.

Lights flash, and they're off.

                                        END SCENE 1.


SCENE 2:

The sofa skids into Steve's living room.

>                    STEVE
>          We made it!

>                    TERRI
>          Are you <u>sure</u> we're in the right year?

Steve looks around, points to the files they were looking through earlier.

>                    STEVE
>          Those are the files we were going over!

>                    TERRI
>          Okay! Everybody, <u>off</u> the sofa!

The all hop off, stunned and amazed.

>                    TERRI (CONT'D)
>               (To Steve)
>          You go find some batteries!

>                    DORA
>          I can do that!
>               (Aside)
>          Can you help me find batteries?

>                    TERRI
>          Oh, no! I think <u>Steve</u> can handle this.

Steve checks the back of the remote.

>                    STEVE
>          Oh, yeah. Good thing I just bought double-
>          A's. I tell ya, the way the kids go through
>          'em, especially after Christmas, with the
>          RC helicopters and the walkie-talkies and
>          the robot dogs --

Terri glares at him.

>                    STEVE (CONT'D)
>          -- I'm gonna run down to my workbench and
>          replace these.

Steve exits.

> TERRI
> Now, all of you just relax. Once we get
> fresh batteries, Steve and I are going to
> have to make a couple more trips to the
> past to get some more characters for this
> year's Avery Play.

> DORA
> What's it about?

> TERRI
> We don't know yet. We're still rounding up
> characters, and our detour to Hamelot cost
> us a bunch of time.

Dora just stares at her, blinking. She waits --

-- and waits --

-- and waits, until --

> DORA
> That sounds great!

Terri looks like her migraine's back. Steve runs in.

> STEVE
> Okay, fresh, new batteries, just out of the
> little package. Man, I hate opening those
> things. You try scissors, and they just get
> stuck, then you practically cut your hand
> open if you use a knife --

Terri's just glaring at him.

> STEVE
> (Finishing quickly)
> But these are new batteries, so we should
> be good this time.

> TERRI
> All of you, stay here and chill. Steve and
> I'll be back in a little bit with some more
> characters.

> STEVE
> Let me get my wife to watch these guys
> while we're gone.
> (Calling)
> Honeeey?!?

                    TERRI
Steve, let's go!

                    STEVE
Honeeey?!?

                    TERRI
Come on, they'll be fine.

                    STEVE
I really need to let her know they're all
here.

                    TERRI
She'll figure it out! We really need to get
going! We've got a lot more time-travelling
to do!

                    STEVE
Okay, there's one way I know to get my wife
to come running --
          (Calling)
Honeeey? Where do we keep the fire
extinguisher?

Honey bursts in instantly, exploding onstage with a huge prop FIRE
EXTINGUISHER. She douses Steve in spray of foam.

                    STEVE (CONT'D)
Do you <u>have</u> to spray me like that <u>every</u>
<u>time</u>? When have I set <u>anything</u> on fire
around here?
(Beat)
Lately?
(Beat)
This week?
(Beat)
Today?
(Beat)
Since lunch?

                    HONEY
See if you can name this tune: "Never mind
the kitchen curtains, put <u>me</u> out!"

                    STEVE
I told you not to lean in like that.

                    HONEY
My left eyebrow <u>still</u> hasn't grown back all
the way.

                    STEVE
Anyway, Honey, we're, uh, rounding up
people for rehearsal and I was wondering
if --

                    TERRI
 -- if you could help us out and play
hostess for everyone here while we go pick
up the rest of the cast.

                    HONEY
I guess I could. Why do they <u>all</u> need a
ride?

                    STEVE
Flat tire.

                    HONEY
Everyone?

                    STEVE
Just the person driving --

                    TERRI
They were all carpooling. We're just going
to run and pick 'em up.

                    HONEY
Oh, I see. I guess so. I'll get a couple
bowls for chips --

                    STEVE
Great!

                    HONEY
-- I know I picked up some dip, and
drinks . . . Oh and nuts --

                    SIR DINTYMOORE
Don't touch his nuts!

                    HONEY
I beg your pardon?

                    TERRI
        (To Honey)
He's just practicing his lines for the
play.

                    HONEY
Lovely.

                    TERRI
Thanks so much!

Terri and Steve start to run off.

                    HONEY
          Oh, but Steve, what happened to the sofa?

                    STEVE
          What do you mean, Honey?

                    HONEY
          Well, earlier I came back in to see if
          there was anything you and Terri needed. I
          guess you two had stepped outside for some
          fresh air --

                    STEVE
          Right!

                    HONEY
          -- maybe to clear your heads --

                    TERRI
          Absolutely!

                    HONEY
          And I noticed the sofa was <u>missing</u> from the
          living room!

                    STEVE
          Yeah, y'see, that's because . . .

                    TERRI
          We took it outside with us.

                    STEVE
          We <u>did</u>?

                    TERRI
          Sure, so we could have someplace
          comfortable to sit outside while we
          worked --

                    HONEY
          But I looked out the window for you.

                    TERRI
          -- while we worked over on the playground
          at Avery.

                    STEVE
          Four-square really helps me think, and I
          need all the help I can get --

                    HONEY
          Yes you do, dear.

                         STEVE
                (Makes a confused face and squints
                 at Honey -- was that a put-down?)
           -- while we . . . hammer out this . . .
      play.
                    (Shakes it off)
      So if the sofa disappears __again__, don't
      __worry__ about it.

He and Terri jump on the sofa.

                         HONEY
      Okay, everyone, I'll be right back out with
      some refreshments.

                         DORA
      Yay!

                         STEVE
                (To Terri)
      Where to next? "Toxic Tale"? "Wizard of
      Webster"? Or one of the really old ones
      like "Kid's Soup" or "A-Haunting We Will
      Go" or "Bermuda Shorts"?

                         TERRI
      Push the button, Steve. I'll tell you on
      the way!

                                        END SCENE 2.


SCENE 3:

Terri and Steve sneak onto the set of "Get a Clue", which looks
suspiciously like Steve's living room redressed and with the stuff
slightly re-arranged.

                         TERRI
      Okay, it's 2004.

                         STEVE
      Right.

                         TERRI
      And this is the set for "Get a Clue."

                         STEVE
      Right again.

                         TERRI
      So where is everyone? Wait -- Steve, we're
      __on__ the set!

STEVE

I think we've established that.

TERRI

We're supposed to be <u>backstage</u>!

STEVE

Uh-oh.

TERRI

The curtain's opening! <u>Hide</u>!

They duck behind a prop door as MAJENTA, MISS SCARLET, MS.WHITE, COLONEL MUSTARD, PROFESSOR PLUMBER, MRS. PEACOCK, NURSE BOMPART, and JEEVES, the butler, who here and now looks surprisingly reminiscent of Riff-Raff from "The Rocky Horror Picture Show".

COLONEL MUSTARD

Yes, Ma'am, we really need that book. It seems to be the only thing missing.

MS. WHITE

Awe you accusing <u>me</u> of something? Am I to be pehsecuted fow weceiving a <u>book</u>?

COLONEL MUSTARD

Well, no Ma'am!

INSPECTOR CLOUSTEAU enters in a blast of "Pink Panther" music.

INSPECTOR CLOUSTEAU

Good evening ladies and gentlemen! Chief Inspector Jacques Clouseau at your service!

COLONEL MUSTARD

I say, where did you come from, old boy?

INSPECTOR CLOUSTEAU

From that *reum* over there.

COLONEL MUSTARD

The what?

INSPECTOR CLOUSTEAU

That *reum*.

The other characters on stage all shrug.

INSPECTOR CLOUSTEAU

Do none of you speak <u>English</u>? That *reum* there! The <u>study</u>!

EVERYBODY
            (Together)
Ohhh.

                    MISS SCARLET
Ooo, you came from the study? How'd you get
in there? Are you imported? Ooo, so many
men, so little time.

                    TERRI
Steve, we have to get out of here!

                    STEVE
But we can't let the audience see we're not
part of the show!

                    TERRI
We'll have to act like we're part of it.

                    STEVE
I don't remember any of my lines from "Get
a Clue" -- that was like five years ago!

                    TERRI
I don't remember mine either. But there is
a show from when I was in high school I
still remember every line from!

                    STEVE
We didn't go to high school together!

                    TERRI
Doesn't matter. Just follow my lead!

                    MISS SCARLET
Who sent for you, Inspector?

                INSPECTOR CLOUSTEAU
Chief Inspector.

                    MISS SCARLET
Chief Inspector. Who called you?

                    JEEVES
I called the inspector.

                INSPECTOR CLOUSTEAU
Chief Inspector. And I have found
Mr. Boddy!

Terri knocks at the door.

The others startle and all turn and stare at the door.

                 COLONEL MUSTARD
              (Out of character, uncertain)
Who . . . who could, uh, that be?

Miss Scarlet shrugs, also out of character.

Jeeves answers the door.

Steve and Terri are standing in the doorway, Terri, wide-eyed, Steve fidgeting and nervous.

> TERRI
>
> It's all right, Janet -- I mean, <u>Steve</u>.

> STEVE
>
> Let's go back. I'm cold and I'm frightened.

> TERRI
>
> Just a moment, Janet, uh, Steve. They may have a telephone.

> JEEVES
>
> Uh, hello?

> TERRI
>
> Oh, uh, ahh . . . <u>Hi</u> there. We're in a bit of a spot. I wonder could you help us -- our car is broken down about two miles back -- Do you have a telephone we might use?

> JEEVES
>
> Yes --

Lightning flashes. Everyone on stage reacts, startled.

> JEEVES (CONT'D)
>
> I think you better both come inside.

> STEVE
>
> You're too kind.

> JEEVES
>
> Wait here.

> TERRI
>
> I'm glad we caught you at home. Uh -- could we use your phone? We're both in a bit of a hurry. We'll just say where we are, then go back to the car -- we don't want to be any worry.

> INSPECTOR CLOUSTEAU
>
> You got caught with a flat. Well, how about that! Well babies, don't you panic.

> STEVE
>
> Terri --

                    TERRI
It's all right, Steve, everything's gonna
be all right. We'll just play along for
now, and we'll pull out the aces when the
time is right.

                    STEVE
This is no time for card tricks, Are you
sure we'll be all right?

                    TERRI
I'm sure, Steve.
          (To the others)
Uh, Hi, there -- I'm Brad, I mean <u>Terri</u>,
this is Steve --

Miss Scarlet sidles up to them.

                    MISS SCARLET
You're very lucky to have found this place
in the dark. With the rain and mist . . .

                    MAGENTA
Yeah -- you're lucky -- I'm lucky -- he's
lucky. We're <u>all</u> lucky . . .

                    MS. WHITE
All except Mr. Boddy.

                    MAGENTA
SHHHHH!!

                    STEVE
Mr. Boddy?

                    MAGENTA
Our host.

                    JEEVES
SHHHHH!!

                    TERRI
          (To Steve)
I <u>knew</u> all those midnight movies in
eleventh grade would pay off one day!

                    JEEVES
Yes, it seems like only yesterday
since . . .

                    TERRI
Since?

                        JEEVES
          It's astounding . . . Time is fleeting.
          Mad-ness . . . takes its toll. But listen
          closely --

                        MAGENTA
          Not for very much longer --

                        JEEVES
          I've got to keep control --



MUSICAL NUMBER:

A dance performance to "The Time Warp"



As the curtain closes, Steve turns to Terri.

                        STEVE
          Whew -- I don't think anyone noticed!

                                        END SCENE 3.

COMMERCIAL

                        ANNOUNCER
          Steve and Terri's Excellent Avery Play
          Adventure will continue, right after this.

A CAVEMAN in a wild wig, thick beard, and club ambles on stage in
front of the curtain. He's wearing a KIRKWOOD HIGH SCHOOL T-SHIRT.

From the opposite direction, his FRIEND saunters over.

                        FRIEND
          Hi, Trag! Why the long face?

                        CAVEMAN
          My son Maurice got in a little fender-
          bender in our new car.

                        FRIEND
          Wow, he's sixteen already?

                        CAVEMAN
          Yeah.

                    FRIEND

Man, they grow up fast -- Hey, he's all
right, isn't he?

                    CAVEMAN

Oh, sure. Just creased the bumper.

                    FRIEND

I bet your premiums are <u>crazy</u>. Teen driver,
male --

                    CAVEMAN

At least we got the "Good Student" and
"Opposable Thumbs" discounts. And I was
just online adjusting our coverage.

                    FRIEND

I <u>hate</u> my insurance company's website. I
can <u>never</u> figure it out.

                    CAVEMAN

Never have any trouble on my insurance
company's website.

                    FRIEND

Who you with?

                    CAVEMAN

Beik-O.

                    FRIEND

Y'know what? I'm gonna check 'em out.

The Friend exits.

                    ANNOUNCER

Beik-O insurance. So simple, even a
<u>Kirkwood</u> graduate can do it!

The Caveman hears this, and insulted and sulking, exits.

                        END COMMERCIAL.


SCENE 4:

Back at Steve's house. It's like the weirdest cocktail party you've
ever seen, with Dora, Annie, Ed, Sir Dintymooore, the cast of "Get a
Clue", LOOMPA-LOOMPAS, PETER PAN, CAPTAIN HOOK, HARRY POTTER, a LUNCH
LADY, THE CAT IN THE HAT, SHAGGY and SCOOBY-DOO, and JIMBO.

Honey is talking to Peter Pan.

                    HONEY

So you were trapped in a <u>peanut</u> butter
<u>jar</u> --

                         PETER PAN
          Yep!

                          HONEY
          And your shadow had to help you escape?

                         PETER PAN
          That's about the size of it!

                          HONEY
          "Return to Neverland" must have been a very
          interesting Avery Play. And that was in
          1989?

                         PETER PAN
          You betcha!

                          HONEY
          Sounds like something they would have done
          in the sixties.

Off to the side, the Cat in the Hat is very studiously licking his
way through a stack of plates on the table. Honey notices this and
runs over to him.

                          HONEY
          What are you doing?!?

                     CAT IN THE HAT
          Helping out with the dishes. Soon as I'm
          done spit-shining these plates, I'll get
          started on the glasses for you.

Honey grabs the plates away from him.

                          HONEY
          That won't be necessary.

                     CAT IN THE HAT
          Fine. Let everyone eat off dirty dishes!

                          HONEY
          We'll use paper.

Nearby, the Lunch Lady shrugs.

                        LUNCH LADY
          That's how we always do 'em at my school.

Over in the corner, Captain Hook talks low with a tiny group of other
characters (Loompa-Loompas, "Get a Clue" cast, whoever), loudly
announcing punchlines.

                       CAPTAIN HOOK
          Rectum? Darn near killed him!

The group around him laughs.

Honey notices someone's behind sticking out from under the refreshment table.

> HONEY
> Who's under the table?

> LUNCH LADY
> I dunno. Some other weird character from one of the Avery Plays. Got all excited when he saw a cheese cube on the floor.

> HONEY
> I didn't put out any <u>cheese</u>.

There's a loud SNAP and a yelp. Jimbo comes out from under the table with a mousetrap closed on his finger.

> JIMBO
> That happens every time I find some cheese!

> HONEY
> That's no weird Avery Play character -- that's my neighbor Jimbo!

> DORA
> You have an <u>elephant</u> for a neighbor?

> HONEY
> I said "Jimbo" not "<u>Jumbo</u>"! Jimbo -- what are you doing in here? You're not in the Avery Play!

> JIMBO
> I just came over to ask Steve if I could borrow some of his tools.

> HONEY
> Sure. Use whatever you want. They're all in <u>your</u> garage.

> CAPTAIN HOOK
> (Suddenly loud)
> And the pirate says "Arrrr, it's drivin' me nuts!"

The group around him laughs.

Sir Dintymoore approaches Honey.

> SIR DINTYMOORE
> Fair Lady! I wouldst have thou knoweth I have valiantly slain the monstrous snake in yon back yard.

                    HONEY
You did <u>what</u>?

                    SIR DINTYMOORE
With mine shining sword, I hacked the
abominable serpent to pieces before it
could do you or your loved ones any harm!

                    HONEY
There's no giant snakes in our yard! There
are no giant snakes in <u>Webster</u> <u>Groves</u>!!

                    JIMBO
Oh, I beg to differ! I was the one who
pointed it out to Sir Beefstew right after
I got here. It was <u>gi-normous</u>! Fifty feet,
at least, and green and coiled all across
your back yard!

                    HONEY
That was our new <u>garden</u> <u>hose</u>!

                    JIMBO
               (To Sir Dintymoore)
That would be why it was sucking on the
<u>spigot</u> for so long.

Harry Potter's talking to the Cat in the Hat.

                    HARRY POTTER
Some people are so blinded by the thirst
for success that it causes them to lose
their values and do things they shouldn't
do.

                    CAT IN THE HAT
Well, that explains the last three "Star
Wars" movies.

Dora's talking to Annie.

                    DORA
Want to hear two short jokes and a long
joke?

                    ANNIE
SURE!

                    DORA
Joke. Joke. Jooooooooooooooooooo
ooooooooooooooookkkkkkkkkkkkkke!

Honey's talking to Miss Scarlet.

                        HONEY
          So I was trying them on and asked, "Steve,
          do these jeans make my butt look like the
          back of our house?" and he said 'No -- "

                        MISS SCARLET
          That's good!

                        HONEY
          He said, "No, the back of the house isn't
          anything <u>close</u> to that color blue!"

                        MISS SCARLET
          I'd call that more <u>thoughtless</u> than mean.

Jimbo overhears.

                        JIMBO
          Mean? I'll tell ya about <u>mean</u>. I got this
          cousin, Cooter. He is so mean, if he
          doesn't like the way you <u>look</u> at him,
          it's --
                    (Points his finger like a gun, makes a blasting
                     noise two or three times)
          Just like that.

                        HONEY
          Oh my goodness! You mean he'd shoot someone
          if he didn't like the way they looked at
          him?

                        JIMBO
          No. He points his finger at you and goes
          (blasting noise).

                        CAPTAIN HOOK
                    (Suddenly loud)
          The chief then declares: "Very well! The
          sentence is death -- by Bongo-Bongo!"

Honey's talking to Dora and Annie.

                        HONEY
          You two couldn't find anything to watch on
          TV?

                        DORA
          Just "The Three Stooges", but we turned it
          off.

                        HONEY
          Yes, I don't like --

                    DORA
        I just wasn't buying Shemp as a surgeon.

Honey does a double-take as the girls walk off.

Mrs. Peacock's talking to Magenta.

                  MRS. PEACOCK
        Excuse me, do you have the time?

                    MAGENTA
        Yes, but not right now.

Magenta walks off.

Col. Mustard's talking to Shaggy.

                    SHAGGY
        No kiddin' man? Like, I love music too! I
        even wrote a song once --

                  COL MUSTARD
        I was a songwriter in my youth, you know --

                    SHAGGY
        -- Except I can't read music, so I don't
        know what the song is, man! Every now and
        then, I hear a cool song on the radio, and
        I, like, wonder if it's the one I
        wrote . . .

                  CAPTAIN HOOK
              (Suddenly loud)
        Walk out? Help me find my keys and we can
        drive out!

The group around him laughs.

There's a flash of light, and Steve and Terri arrive, the sofa
sliding into the middle of the room, a couple more characters
including MRS. CLAMCHOWDER on board. Everyone hops off.

Mrs. Clamchowder explodes with her awkward, crazy
gymnastics/dance/martial arts move. While she heaves, out of breath,
everyone backs away uncertainly.

                    HONEY
        Steve, I think you need to explain this
        whole sofa thing to me again.

                    TERRI
        Looks like we've got enough to do a show
        now!

                    STEVE
        I've been thinking Terri --

                    TERRI
        Uh-oh!

                    STEVE
         -- and I've got an idea.

                    HONEY
        Where's the fire extinguisher?!?

                    STEVE
        We've got lots of material, but nothing
        new!

                    TERRI
        That was the whole point of travelling back
        in time.

                    STEVE
        But if I go forward in time, I can get
        something the audience hasn't seen yet!

                    TERRI
        We don't --

Steve hops on the sofa.

                    STEVE
        I'll be right back!

He hits the button on the remote, and he's gone.

                    TERRI
                (To Honey)
        So how's it goin'?

No one notices the MUMMY laying on the floor where the sofa was.

                    HONEY
        I think Steve'll be sitting out the play
        next year.

                    TERRI
        Puhh -- him and me both after this!

Dora notices the Mummy as it starts to get up. She points,
stuttering.

                    DORA
        M-muh --!

                    CAPTAIN HOOK
                  (Suddenly loud)
          So the kid finally looks back at the driver
          and says, "Look, mister, I'm not a welder!"

The group around him laughs.

                    DORA
          ¡Momia! (mo-mee-ah!)

                    TERRI
          What?

                    DORA
          Mummy!

                    TERRI
          Ahh, it must've gotten stuck under the sofa
          when we made that second pass through "Lost
          at Avery"!

Everyone shouts and scatters and makes for curtains and doors as
"Yakkity Sax" comes up. They all begin ducking in and out of doors,
curtains, until, at last, they shut the Mummy in a closet.

Honey glares at Terri.

                    TERRI
          We'll get that  . . . later!

Lights flash. The sofa skids into the room, Steve, JACK SPARROW,
INDIANA JONES, CLAUDIA, and a CHORUS OF FRANKENSTEIN MONSTERS on
board. They all start unpiling awkwardly from the sofa, the Monsters
particularly clumsy.

                    TERRI
          Jack Sparrow, Indiana Jones, Claudia -- and
          a chorus of Frankenstein monsters?!? What
          kind of play has all them in it?!?

Jack Sparrow spies Captain Hook in the corner --

                    JACK SPARROW
          Dad!

-- and runs over to him with a hug, joining the group Captain Hook's
telling jokes to.

                    CLAUDIA
          I don't know why you guys grabbed me! I was
          home taking care of my baby -- I'm not even
          in the Avery Play!

                         TERRI
          Steve, why would you bring back these,
          these . . . <u>Monsters</u>?!?

                         STEVE
          Monsters? Oh, you may <u>think</u> they're
          shambling, clumsy brutes. But they're
          really advanced, and sophisticated . . .
          <u>men</u> <u>about</u> <u>town</u>!

Canes are tossed to Steve and the Monsters from OS and Steve grabs a
top hat.


MUSICAL NUMBER:

A dance performance to "Puttin' on the Ritz" *Young Frankenstein*-style


                         TERRI
          Yeah, okay, the monsters are in.

                         STEVE
          Hey, Claudia, could you keep an eye on them
          for us?

                         CLAUDIA
          No way! They're horrible! Scary!

                         TERRI
          Claudia, just . . . take charge of them,
          wouldja? Please?

                         CLAUDIA
          Fine. I'll "monstersit".
                    (To the Monsters)
          Shamble over here, er, Frank and Frank and
          Frank . . .

They shamble to her. She starts to lead them off stage. The Monsters
grunt and grumble.

                         CLAUDIA (CONT'D)
          So, why don't you guys tell me a little
          about yourselves?

They exit.

                         CLAUDIA (OS)
                 (Belting it out like Madeline Kahn)
         O-o-o-oh! Sweet Mystery of Life at last
         I've <u>found</u> you!!

Everyone on stage does a startle- or a double-take, with a mixture of
amused and frightened faces.

                         TERRI
         Uh-oh! Look at the time!

                         STEVE
         We gotta get over to Steger Auditorium and
         get <u>everything</u> set up <u>now</u>!
                 (To the whole group)
         Everybody, everybody, listen up! We have to
         go! Now!

                         TERRI
                 (To Steve)
         We'll put some in your car, and some in my
         car!

                         DORA
         Why didn't you take everyone straight to
         the stage at Steger in the first place?

Terri and Steve look at each other, and then go back to panicking.

                         STEVE
         Sure, <u>now</u> we get suggestions!
                 (To the whole group)
         Everybody just start piling in my car, and
         when no more fit, start getting in Terri's!

Everyone starts to rush offstage. The last to go are Honey, Captain
Hook, and his group.

                         STEVE (OS)
         We can just tie some of those Frankenstein
         Monsters to the roof!

Captain Hook's group starts heading off. Captain Hook shouts,
finishing his punchline as he runs after them all.

                         CAPTAIN HOOK
                 (Hurrying)
         . . . So he tells her, "I didn't know I'd
         be performing in a <u>cathedral</u>!"


                                        END SCENE 4.

SCENE 5:

Backstage at Steger. The sounds of big laughs and big enthusiastic applause.

                    TERRI
          We did it, Steve!

                    STEVE
          It actually worked! Everybody loves it! <u>All</u>
          the characters -- Dora --

                    TERRI
          -- The Frankenstein Monsters --

                    STEVE
          -- The Cat in the Hat -- Even that knight,
          and he was an <u>accident</u>! We're a hit!

                    TERRI
          I can't believe it!

                    DR. SMITH (OS)
          I can!

Steve and Terri whirl to see DR. SMITH appear in a cloud of weird smoke. He has a huge "Doc Brown" white wig, goggles, a futuristic silvery suit and a glowing tie.

                    STEVE & TERRI
                    (Together)
          Dr. Smith!

                    STEVE
          See? His suit's all -- and his
          hair -- wearing a tie that's . . .

                    TERRI
                    (Poking Steve)
          Focus!
                    (To Dr. Smith)
          There's something <u>different</u> about you . . .

                    DR. SMITH
          I'm not the Dr. Smith you know. I'm from
          the <u>future</u>.

                    TERRI & STEVE
                    (Together)
          The future?

                    DR. SMITH
          From the year 2049, where I'm still
          principal of Avery after forty more years.

                         (Aside)
I _love_ this school!

                DR. SMITH (CONT'D)
             (To Steve and Terri)
We just had the 100th anniversary Avery
Play, and it's the biggest hit ever --

                STEVE
But why are you here? Now?

                DR. SMITH
Trying to fix things. The sixtieth
anniversary show was pretty . . . lame. You
guys messed it up big time.

                TERRI
So you travelled back in time and gave
Steve the bag of videos and that time-
travel remote so we could put together a
better review show!

                STEVE
Why didn't you just tell us?

                DR. SMITH
An Avery Play's like homework -- you have
to figure it out for yourself.

                STEVE & TERRI
             (Together)
Yeah.

                DR. SMITH
I was hoping you two could work out a
better show. And you did! Steve, I don't
know why everyone says you're such a boob!

                STEVE
Thanks a lot, Dr. Smith. I was getting
pretty worried when -- Who says I'm a
boob?!?

                DR. SMITH
But there's one thing I need to know before
I go back to the future.

                STEVE
Yeah?

                DR. SMITH
What's your big finale?

                    STEVE
What else after all this? We're doing "The
Time Warp" --

                    TERRI & STEVE
          (Aside, together)
-- Again!


MUSICAL NUMBER:

A reprise of "The Time Warp" number, only with the ENTIRE CAST on
stage.


                    STEVE
So, Terri, what do you want to do for next
year's show?

                    TERRI
Let someone else produce it!


                                        END SCENE 5.

                                        END ACT TWO.

                                        CURTAIN.


                        THE END

whatever.

# WHATEVER (2010)

*With sales at her "Whatever" shop down and bills piling up, busy Avery mom Mickie finds herself in trouble — because they live upstairs from the shop, going out of business won't cost just her job, but their home as well! Trying to keep it all secret from her guitarist husband Stan and their kids Partario and Lulu, she enlists her best friend and neighbor Viv to concoct scheme after wacky scheme to raise the money.*

*Meanwhile, the busy life of an Avery parent swirls around her as Partario tries to get an act ready for Razzmatazz (no easy thing entering a talent show with no talent!) while Lulu searches for just the right experiment for the Science Fair. And then there's Stan, racing around with Viv's retired British rocker husband Foz to arrange a special birthday surprise for Mickie's—gasp—fortieth. But when Mickie and Viv accidentally eavesdrop on the two and misunderstand their plans—well, as they say in* TV Guide, *"hilarity ensues."*

FOR OUR LONG-SUFFERING AND BELEAGUERED PRODUCER—AND NOW DIRECTOR—TERRI, "WHATEVER" had become a mantra and sometime battlecry during the production of *Steve and Terri's Excellent Avery Play Adventure*. Some of the staging was a bit complicated, and availability of actors and actresses for the anniversary show waxed and waned in the weeks of rehearsals leading up to the performances. Each bit of bad news was met simply with a shake of her head and an uttered "whatever" until one night, after four or five problems hit one on top of the other, her "whatevers" started her laughing at the absurdity of it all.

"That's the title of next year's show," I told her.

Months later, when it came time to commence work on the new Avery Play I also promised her an easier show to stage. "Think of it like an old episode of *The Honeymooners* or *I Love Lucy*, one set and four main characters, with a few others coming and going as needed." I assured her the difficulties of the last show would be minimized in this one with so many fewer moving parts. With the model set, I began to outline the story, calling back to the classic TV comedies I'd mentioned, with their couples working in crossed plots with eavesdropping and misunderstandings and slapstick bits. Plus, the single set approach allowed the creation of a much more elaborate set, with more depth, detail, and personality (though the Whatever shop owed more in appearance to *Sanford & Son* than *The Honeymooners* when finished) that gave the show a certain richness in appearance we hadn't seen in the last few plays.

Unlike the mash-ups of previous years, this story would feature a cast of original characters. Hands down, my favorite to write that year was Foz. The addled British ex-rocker was a perfect channel for all manner of confusion, incomprehension and forgetfulness jokes. Coupled with a spot-on accent and outrageous 80s rocker costumes, of all the characters that year, he was the biggest hit with the audiences in each performance and earned Jon, the actor portraying him, the coveted Ham award from the rest of the cast for going most over the top.

*Whatever* also marked my stepping up my involvement in the show. Co-directing with Terri, I was able to coach the actors through some of the gags and bits, getting them closer to what I'd envisioned. But I was also able to listen and watch as they all rehearsed, and many of the best one-liners and throwaways were bits we incorporated from the actors' improvisations or attempts to break one another up at practice. It was magical to see the plain, black-and white-words I put on paper brought to breathing, full-color life, with all the detail and silliness I pictured and sometimes heading off in a direction of its own. Kids in the audience really connected with this one. I'm not exactly sure why. Maybe it was the family-and-kids characters or the parent struggling to hold a business together, but they all laughed loud at the funny parts, shouted at the stage to warn characters in other parts, and got really quiet at the one worrisome part. That was the best part for me—watching the story really grab the audience and hold them until the final curtain. Whatever? Hardly.

"WHATEVER"


Written by

*Patrick Dorsey*

## "WHATEVER"

CHARACTERS:

MICKIE PUCKETT, an Avery mom running her "Whatever" shop.

VIV FOZZARD, her neighbor and cohort.

STAN PUCKETT, Mickie's guitarist husband.

FOZ FOZZARD, Viv's out-of-it husband who vaguely remembers being a British rock star once.

LULU, Mickie and Stan's scientastic daughter.

PARTARIO, Mickie and Stan's showbiz-wannabe son.

ELVIRA, Viv and Foz's DD and Lulu's BFF.

THE PTO CHAIR to help the teachers.

TEACHERS, because every school has them.

DR. WIDGET, the new school district superintendent.

a KIRKWOOD STUDENT, in the wrong neighborhood.

THE GUYS IN THE BAND, playin' at music.

GUY ST. GUY, a gameshow host.

THE LOVELY VELMA, his always-lovely assistant.

a REPORTER to tell the story.

a PHOTOGRAPHER, to take some pictures.

NURSE AHAB, the new Avery School Nurse.

SWINE FLU PATIENTS, under-the-weather thrillers.

VAL, the totally tubular babysitter.

HEATHER, Val's car-troubled friend.

JEFF ALBERTSON, collector of all things collectible.

"WHATEVER"

ACT ONE


SCENE 1:

The WHATEVER SHOP, a boutique full of shelves, knickknacks, holistic medicine supplies, and well, whatever.

TEACHER 1, TEACHER 2, TEACHER 3, and THE PTO CHAIR are all shopping.

                    TEACHER 1
          Wow -- an everything shop.

                    TEACHER 2
          I think it's a whatever shop.

                    TEACHER 3
          What's the difference?

                    TEACHER 2
          Well, an everything shop would have
          everything. A whatever shop has (looking
          around) . . . whatever.

Teacher 1 squints, not buying it.

                    TEACHER 3
          What a funny old Crackerjack box.

                    TEACHER 1
          The nice part is, this place is so close to
          Avery.

                    TEACHER 2
          I know! If there's anything I need real
          quick for my class, I can duck over here
          and be back in no time! Oooh, look at this!

She pulls a bizarre LAMP made from a worn out, oversized stuffed animal with a lampshade over its head. She turns it on and it lights up.

                    TEACHER 3
          This is just the thing for my reading
          corner!

                    TEACHER 1
          To keep the kids from spending too much
          time in it?

MICKIE, Avery mom and owner of the shop, enters.

                    MICKIE
          If there's anything you need, just let me
          know. We've got pretty much -- whatever --
          you want.

She smiles, nods, trying to get everyone to react to the joke, but
they're not buying it.

                    PTO CHAIR
          So, are you in charge of that special event
          fundraiser again this year?

                    MICKIE
          Oh, no, my neighbor Viv drew the short
          straw on that one -- I mean, she's chairing
          the committee.

                    PTO CHAIR
          I hear she has something different in mind
          for this year.

                    MICKIE
          Dunno. The only thing I heard about was her
          husband Foz's suggestion for an exhibition
          boxing match --

                    PTO CHAIR
          They can't do that with parents!

                    MICKIE
          No, with one of the kids --

                    PTO CHAIR
          We can't have two students fighting!

                    MICKIE
          -- Not two kids -- one kid and a kangaroo.

Everyone stares at her.

                    PTO CHAIR
          Ohh, I've met Foz -- he's Elvira's father,
          isn't he?

Mickie nods, the teachers nodding along.

                    PTO CHAIR (CONT'D)
          Say no more.

The PTO Chair turns, trips over whatever, and falls to the floor,
knocked out.

Everyone hovers, unsure.

                    TEACHER 1
        Call someone!

                    MICKIE
        We need a doctor!
              (Aside)
        Is there a doctor in the house?

Out in the audience, DR. WIDGET, the new superintendent, jumps to
her feet.

                    DR. WIDGET
              (Heroic)
        I'm a doctor!

                TEACHER 1, 2, 3 & MICKIE
              (Together)
        Dr. Widget, our new superintendent!

She rushes through the audience and springs confidently on stage.

She kneels down over the PTO Chair. She takes her pulse, puts an ear
to her chest.

                    TEACHER 3
        Is everything Okay?

                    DR. WIDGET
        I don't know . . . I'm not that kind of a
        doctor . . .

Rimshot.

PTO Chair sits up.

                    PTO CHAIR
        Hey, that was Dr. Doe's joke!

                    DR. WIDGET
        Well, I found it in the office when I moved
        in, and it's my joke now!

                    PTO CHAIR
        Oh, look at the time!

                    DR. WIDGET
        Yikes!

They all head for the door. As they leave, VIV enters.

                    PTO CHAIR
              (To Viv)
        Tell your husband good luck with the
        kangaroo!

They exit.

                         VIV
                   (To Mickie)
            You told them about that?

                         MICKIE
            It just came up!

                         VIV
            How does kangaroo boxing just "come up"?

                         MICKIE
            Oh, whatever.

She sinks to the floor and sits with her face in her hands.

                         VIV
            Hey, are you okay?

                         MICKIE
            I am. It's just . . .

                         VIV
            It's just -- ?

                         MICKIE
            It's just the shop --

Mickie gets up and starts dusting and arranging things.

                         VIV
            I can see how in six months this place can
            get a little overwhelming.

                         MICKIE
            Ten months, actually.

                         VIV
            Wow. Almost a year since you left your old
            job to open the shop?

                         MICKIE
            I knew it would be rough, but --

                         VIV
            But?

                         MICKIE
            Oh, Viv, sales have never been good! And
            lately they've gotten worse, and if they
            don't turn around soon, we're gonna lose
            the whole place!

                         VIV
            But you live upstairs! If you lose the
            shop --

MICKIE

I know.

VIV

What's Stan had to say?

MICKIE

Not much. He's been busy with Foz and their band and playing gigs evenings and weekends.

VIV

He had to know the risk of opening a shop like this.

MICKIE

Sure he did.

VIV

And how things are if sales have been so low.

MICKIE

Sure . . . if I told him.

VIV

You haven't told him?!?

MICKIE

I've been meaning to!

VIV

You can't hide this!

MICKIE

I'll think of something.

VIV

Oh no. The last time you said that was at Halloween when we ran out of candy for the trick-or-treaters.

MICKIE

I took care of it.

VIV

You handed out Canadian postage stamps, extension cords, and thongs!

MICKIE

Well, in my defense, in these old Webster houses, you can never have too many extension cords. And some of those girls who came to the door were . . . barefoot.

                          VIV
          Mickie, you've got to tell him.

                          MICKIE
          Not just yet. I'm not that far behind with
          the bills. If I can just come up with
          something --

                          VIV
          Like what? I know you, Mickie -- if you're
          far enough behind to be worried, you're not
          going to just dig what you need out of your
          sofa cushions in lost change.

Mickie pulls out her cell phone

                          MICKIE
          Hey, there's that new TV game show I heard
          about, the one where you call and sign up
          and they randomly stop at your house and
          ask you questions for prizes!

                          VIV
          The chances of your ending up on that are
          like a zillion to one!

                          MICKIE
          Better odds than I've got right now!

Mickie starts dialing

                          VIV
          And what if you don't win? You really
          should tell Stan.

                          MICKIE
          You don't tell Foz everything.

                          VIV
          Oh, yes I do . . . he just doesn't remember
          things.

                          MICKIE
          Whatever.

Their kids, PARTARIO, LULU, and ELVIRA come in wearing school
backpacks.

                          MICKIE
          Oh good, it's ringing.

                          VIV
          Hi, Elvira! Lulu! Partario!

                    LULU
Hi, Mom!

                    ELVIRA
H-A-K, M-D!

Mickie starts to ask Viv.

                    VIV
               (To Mickie)
"Hugs and kisses, mother dear." That kid
spends so much time texting, she's <u>thinking</u>
in abbreviations now.
               (To Elvira)
How was school sweetheart?

                    ELVIRA
O -- M -- G!

                    LULU
We had swine flu shots today. And that new
school nurse isn't right!

                    MICKIE
               (To Viv)
It picked up (Beat) It's some automated
voice mail thing --

                    PARTARIO
Mom!

                    MICKIE
               (Into the phone)
Yes, Mickie Puckett --

                    PARTARIO
Mom!

                    MICKIE
707 --

                    PARTARIO
Mo-om!

                    MICKIE
Marshall Avenue --

                    PARTARIO
               (Funny voice)
Mom! Mom!

                    MICKIE
Webster Groves --

                        PARTARIO
Mmmmmmmmom!

                        MICKIE
Missouri --

                        PARTARIO
Momomomomomomom!

                        MICKIE
63119 -- Partario, what!!!

                        PARTARIO
I want to show you this really cool idea IO
had for the Razzmatazz talent show at
school!

                        MICKIE
That's months away -- you couldn't have
waited five seconds?

                        PARTARIO
No.

                        MICKIE
Whatever.

                        PARTARIO
Okay, check this out: I have these tools --

He pulls a HAMMER, WRENCH, BIG TAPE MEASURE and a LARGE SCREWDRIVER
from his backpack.

                        MICKIE
Son, I don't think you can build anything
on stage in the time they give for --

Partario shoves them all in her arms.

                        PARTARIO
I'm not building anything --

He steps back.

                        PARTARIO (CONT'D)
I'm going to juggle them --

                        MICKIE
I don't think that's such a good idea --

Partario pulls a long bandana from his backpack.

                        PARTARIO
  -- Blindfolded!

He starts tying it around his head, over his eyes.

>                    MICKIE
>          I think I'm really going to have to say no
>          on this one.

>                    PARTARIO
>          I've been practicing! Developed my other
>          senses like Daredevil in the comic books!
>          Throw them to me -- you'll see!

He holds his arms out, bouncing, ready.

Mickie throws each of the tools to him one at a time

- Bang!

- Clang!

- Clunk!

- Sp-tang!

They all bounce right off his head.

The moms look horrified, the girls terribly bored. A smile spreads over Partario's blindfolded face as he nods, proud.

>                    PARTARIO
>          That's what I'm talkin' about!

Grinning, he holds his hand up for a high-five. Mickie shrugs and tries to give him one, but his hand misses hers, and they end up swatting each other in the forehead.

>                    MICKIE
>          Don't you have homework to get to?!?

>                    LULU
>          First he has to help me with my Science
>          Fair project. Elvira's helping, too.

>                    MICKIE
>          If it's all right with Mrs. Fozzard . . .

>                    VIV
>          Ah, it's science fair. Get to work!

The kids gather up their stuff.

>                    MICKIE
>          It's so great that our daughters are such
>          good friends!

>                    ELVIRA
>          B-F-Fs 4 E-V-A!

The kids run through the back door.

                    MICKIE
But I really hope Lulu doesn't pick that up
from Elvira.

                    VIV
You and me both -- It's like living in the
*Da Vinci Code* trying to decipher what she's
saying all the time!
          (Reaches in her pocket)
I have to keep notecards!

FOZ stumbles in the front door. With long hair and the costume of an
80s rocker, he's slow, shambling, a touch confused by the door's
action.

                    VIV (CONT'D)
Foz, we're over here!

                    FOZ
'ello my pet!

                    MICKIE
The girls and Partario just went upstairs.

                    FOZ
I 'aven't seen your other kids around in a
while.

                    MICKIE
We only have the two, Foz -- Lulu and
Partario.

                    FOZ
No, the <u>little</u> one. Skinny, big eyes,
with --
          (Mimes something from his back)
Always runnin' all over the place and
hiding. The little furry fella.

                    MICKIE
You mean our <u>cat</u>?

                    FOZ
And the long, windy chap? With the one
fancy leather stocking --

                    MICKIE
Partario's pet snake.

Foz squints, thinking hard.

                    FOZ
Riiiiiiight . . . .

                    MICKIE
We haven't --

                    FOZ
  . . . Riiiiiiight . . . .

                    MICKIE
Looking for Stan?

                    FOZ
Actually, I was lookin' for <u>Stan</u>. I was
supposed to meet him and the fellas here to
play.

                    MICKIE
(Beat) Yeah, he's in the back room, waxin'
his --

Viv looks at her as STAN comes in from the back room, a shiny golf
putter in one hand and a can of Turtlewax in the other.

                    STAN
    See, Mickie, I told you this putter would
    look like new after a good buffing.

She takes it from him and examines it.

                    MICKIE
Huh. Look at that.

She tosses it absentmindedly over in a pile of whatever, then sidles
over next to Viv.

                    MICKIE (CONT'D)
    Listen, Honey, Viv and I have to run a
    quick errand.

                    STAN
That's okay. We'll be here with the band.
We have that gig tonight, but it's not 'til
later.

                    VIV
That's right -- that big-deal music
critic's going to there!

                    FOZ
Ahh, critics -- like they know anything. My
old band's first review said we'd never be
remembered.

                    VIV
And what was the name of that band?

                    FOZ
I don't remember.
          (To Stan)
No worries, squire. We'll have an
absolutely brill show tonight, a real
banger that'll leave that critic completely
knackered!

                    STAN
I never know <u>what</u> he's saying, but it
always sounds good.

                    MICKIE
          (Hurried)
Great! Come on, Viv.

                    VIV
What are we doing?

                    MICKIE
You remember.

                    VIV
No, I really don't --

Mickie surreptitiously kicks her.

                    VIV (CONT'D)
Oww! No, I really don't --

Mickie kicks her again.

                    VIV (CONT'D)
<u>Oww</u>! This doesn't help, Mickie, I've tried
it on Foz.

                    MICKIE
The project we were talking about earlier?

                    STAN
The fundraiser?

                    MICKIE
It <u>is</u> a fund-raiser . . .

                    VIV
          (Getting it finally and playing along)
Oh, that. What are we doing?

                    MICKIE
Just come on.

She hustles her to the door.

VIV

How am I supposed to know what your
suddenly brilliant idea is?

MICKIE

Whatever.

Mickie and Viv exit.

FOZ

Shame, really, the way Viv 'as trouble
remembering things that way.

THE GUYS FROM THE BAND enter, looking like a mix of leftovers from
Spinal Tap, ZZ Top, or whatever other bands.

STAN

Oh, guys, great! I was starting to worry
whether you were coming or not!

BAND GUY #1

You kiddin'? We're still playing, right?

STAN

For sure!

BAND GUY #2

Then what are we waiting for?

FOZ

I'll turn on the telly!

They all reach around various corners of the room and produce GUTAR
HERO and BAND HERO instruments.

STAN

Power up the Wii and let's do this thing!

MUSICAL NUMBER:

A dance performance to "Jump"

STAN

That was awesome, guys! A little playing
always takes the edge off before a show!

The Guys From The Band all start filing out.

                    STAN (CONT'D)
          All right, I'll see everyone at the gig
          tonight.

The Guys From The Band all wave and exit the front door.

                    FOZ
          I love that game. Don't know why,
          really . . . reminds me of something from
          when I was younger, I guess . . .

                    STAN
          Foz, listen, while we've got some time
          here -- I need your help.

                    FOZ
          With what?

                    STAN
          In a couple days it's Mickie's birthday,
          and I'm trying to come up with a big
          surprise for her -- it's her fortieth.

DRAMATIC CUE SOUND: *Dun-Dun-Duuuuun!*

Foz looks around, wondering where the dramatic music came from.

                    FOZ
          Oh, that's swee' o' you. A special birthday
          for when she turns for'y.

DRAMATIC CUE SOUND: *Dun-Dun-Duuuuun!*

Foz reacts, hearing it again.

                    FOZ
          Where's that comin' from?

                    STAN
          I want to surprise her -- as busy as we've
          been with the band, I'm sure she thinks I'm
          clueless about her birthday. I've got some
          ideas --

                    FOZ
          You leave it to me, squire --

                    STAN
          Foz, you're a great guy, but no way.

> > FOZ
> > (Like he didn't hear Stan)
>
> -- when confronted wif a challenge, you
> gotta emulate the great minds of the past
> and ask yourself, "What would MacGyver do?
> What would the A-Team do?" --

> > STAN
>
> On second thought, maybe I'll just --

> > FOZ
>
> -- and you draw up a plan.

Stan does a double-take.

> > STAN
>
> Foz, that was unexpectedly downright
> coherent.

> > FOZ
>
> Thank you!

Foz goes to one of the counters, pulls out a large sheet of paper,
and hunches over it carefully, drawing something out of sight of the
audience.

Stan paces, thinking out loud.

> > STAN
>
> Okay, a plan . . . I was thinking maybe
> dinner out someplace nice, but that didn't
> seem special enough.

> > FOZ
> > (Still drawing)
>
> Riiight.

> > STAN
>
> So then I was thinking of maybe something
> at one of the clubs we play at, surprise
> her and have the band play for her and
> spotlight her, but she hates when she has
> everyone looking at her, especially when
> there's not a lot of people she knows.

> > FOZ
> > (Still drawing)
>
> Riiight.

> STAN

And then I thought of a surprise party,
have all our friends over. But those get so
clichéd, with the black balloons and
tombstone decorations. And somebody always
blows the secret and ruins the surprise.

> FOZ
> (Still drawing)

Riiight.

He heads over to Foz.

> STAN

Man, you've really been at it -- What did
you come up with?
> (Leans over, interested)

Hey, these are just pictures of duckies!!

He grabs the oversized sheets, holds them up so the audience can see
the cartoon ducks drawn all over.

> FOZ

I like duckies.

> STAN

I take back everything I said. Come on,
Foz. You need to look at what's really
going on -- this is like over the summer,
when you thought Mr. Teitelbaum up the
street was building a death ray machine in
his yard.

> FOZ

He was!

> STAN

It was a heater for his swimming pool.

> FOZ

He doesn't have a swimming pool.

> STAN

It was right next to the pool heater he was
building.

> FOZ

Riiiight. (Beat) Riiiight. Can we go over
and go swimming, then?

He kicks off his shoes, starts undoing his pants.

                    STAN

      Whoa, whoa . . . I have no idea why you'd
      have a swimsuit on under there right now,
      but I don't want to find out for sure.
      You're always welcome in my home, Foz, but
      this is a <u>family</u> show.

There's a knock at the door.

                 STAN (CONT'D)
      Who'd be knocking on the door to the shop?

Lulu and Elvira lead Partario in from the back room, Partario decked
out in a strange HEADBAND and HARNESS arrangement with WIRES AND
FLASHING LIGHTS all over.

                   LULU
      Hi, Daddy!

                   FOZ
      I'll get it.

Foz goes to the door while the kids gather near Stan.

                   LULU
      I want to show you my project for the
      science fair!

Stan looks over Partario, concerned.

                   STAN
      You didn't get this idea from Mr. Fozzard,
      did you?

                   LULU
      Nope, it's all my idea.

Foz opens the door and a KIRKWOOD STUDENT in a Kirkwood High School
T-Shirt is standing there.

                 KIRKWOOD STUDENT
        (Obviously reading from his clipboard, poorly)
      Hello, sir or madam, I am part of a.
      Fundraising effort for. Your High School
      Name -- Kirkwood High School. And we're
      selling these very valuable. Kirkwood
      entertainment coupon books --

                   FOZ
      Ha! You're not foolin' me -- there's
      nothing entertain' in <u>Kirkwood</u>!

He pushes the Student out and closes the door on him. He rejoins Stan
and the kids.

Lulu arranges Elvira and Partario and begins "presenting", reading from a stack of index cards.

> LULU
> I'm exploring whether positive reinforcement or negative reinforcement works better in learning a task. My subjects are each trying to memorize a poem. On the positive reinforcement side, Elvira will be given her favorite treat -- a Girl Scout Thin Mint cookie -- every time she reaches a predetermined point in the poem "Green Eggs and Ham" with no error.

> ELVIRA
> "Green Eggs and Ham" by Dr. Seuss.

SOUND EFFECTS: A pleasant *DING*.

In a very girl-being-overly-pleasant-with-her-friend way, Lulu hands Elvira a cookie, Lulu takes a bite and continues.

> ELVIRA (CONT'D)
> I am Sam
> Sam I am
> That Sam-I-am!
> That Sam-I-am!
> I do not like that Sam-I-am!

*DING!* Lulu gives Elvira another cookie

> ELVIRA (CONT'D)
> Do you like
> green eggs and ham?
> I do not like them, Sam-I-am.
> I do not like
> green eggs and ham.
> Would you like them
> here or there?
> I would not like them
> here or there.
> I would not like them anywhere.
> I do not like
> green eggs and ham.
> I do not like them, Sam-I-am.

*DING!* Lulu tosses the cookie to Elvira, who catches it in her mouth, snapping it out of the air like a dog with a treat.

>                    LULU
> On the negative reinforcement side, my
> brother Partario will receive an electric
> shock every time he makes a mistake
> reciting Edgar Alan Poe's poem "The Raven"

>                    PARTARIO
> Once upon a midnight dreary, while I
> pondered, weak and weary --

SOUND EFFECTS: An awful BUZZ. Partario shakes.

>                    PARTARIO (CONT'D)
> Oww! But that's how it starts!

>                    LULU
> You forgot the title and author.

>                    PARTARIO
> "The Raven," by Edgar Alan Poe.
> Once upon a midnight dreary, as I pondered,
> weak and weary --

*BUZZ!* He's shocked again.

>                    PARTARIO (CONT'D)
> Owww!

>                    LULU
> It's "while I pondered."

>                    PARTARIO
> "The Raven," by Edgar Alan Poe.
> Once upon a midnight dreary, while I
> pondered, weak and weary --

*BUZZ!* He's shocked again.

>                    PARTARIO (CONT'D)
> Owww! I said while.

>                    LULU
> My finger slipped.

>                    PARTARIO
> "The Raven," by Edgar Alan Poe.
> Once upon a midnight dreary, while I
> pondered, weak and weary --

He pauses, wincing, expecting a shock, then goes on.

>                    PARTARIO (CONT'D)
> -- Over many a quaint and curious volume of
> forgotten lore,

                    PARTARIO (CONT'D)
          While I nodded, nearly napping, suddenly
          there came a tapping,
          As of some one gently rapping, rapping at
          my chamber door.

Elvira reaches over and pushes the shock button on Lulu's remote.

*BUZZ!*

                    PARTARIO (CONT'D)
          Cut it out!

                    ELVIRA
          R-O-T-F-L!

*BUZZ!* She shocks him again.

Partario grabs at the remote, but instead gets Lulu's arm.

Giggling, Elvira hits the button again. *BUZZ!* Partario and Lulu are
both shocked.

                    LULU
          Oww! Cut it out, Elvira!

They slap fight for the remote, ending up in a tangle. Partario gets
hold of the remote, and with both girls making contact with him,
holds it up.

                    PARTARIO
          Let's see how you two like it!

He triumphantly pushes the button.

*BUZZ!* All three kids are shocked.

                    STAN
                 (Aside)
          Didn't see that one comin'!

He picks up the remote.

                    STAN (CONT'D)
          Partario, take that stuff off. Lulu, you
          can't do your experiment with your brother.

                    LULU
          But why not?

                    FOZ
          For one thing, the N of your sample is way
          too low for any sta'istical significance.

                    FOZ (CONT'D)
     An' your subjects -- one's in fif' grade,
     one's in second, one's a boy and one's a
     girl -- and don't even get me star'ed on
     the variance in rhythm and vocabulary
     between the two sample pieces --

                    STAN
     Foz, how do you know all that?

                    FOZ
     One thing I know thing or two about, it's
     electro-shock.

                    STAN
     Come on, let's go find something fun to do.

He leads the group out the back door.


                                        END SCENE 1.

MUSICAL NUMBER:

A dance performance to "Shock The Monkey"


SCENE 2:

Mickie and Viv enter the shop in clown wigs and noses, handcuffed
together.

                    VIV
     I told you we'd never make any money like
     that.

                    MICKIE
     Not with us both dressed like clowns! If
     you'd worn the gorilla costume like I
     suggested --

                    VIV
     Oh, no. That thing smelled like moldy old
     carpeting and feet! Besides, that plan was
     like something from an old TV show or an
     Avery play.

They both glance at the audience and shrug.

                    MICKIE
     Whatever. (Beat) Oh, what am I going to do,
     Viv?

They yank off the noses and wigs.

                         VIV
               You could try, oh, I don't know, telling
               Stan.

                         MICKIE
               I can't.

                         VIV
               Where is Stan, anyway?

                         MICKIE
               Oh, he's probably in the back playing with
               his one-eyed --.

                         STAN (OS)
               Raaaahr!

Stan backs through the door, waving a large STUFFED CYCLOPS TOY.

                         STAN
               Boy, this monster's fun!

Still with his back to the shop, he tosses the toy away and calls to
the back room.

                         STAN (CONT'D)
               Okay, kids, you finish eating and we'll be
               back in a minute -- Foz and I just have to
               run next door to his house.

Mickie jumps.

                         MICKIE
               He can't see us like this -- he'll know
               something's up!

                         VIV
               Ya think?

                         MICKIE
               Hide!

They both take off in opposite directions, then are jerked back to
the middle of the room by their handcuffs. They scramble around on
the floor, the handcuffs creating problems as they try to get up or
head in different directions.

                         MICKIE (CONT'D)
               Under the table!

They scrabble on all fours to a table and hide under it just as Stan
and Foz come in from the back.

                         STAN
          Hey, Foz, I just had an idea!

                         FOZ
          What's that?

Stan glances around as the women peek out and then duck back again.

                         STAN
          Well, remember what we were talking about
          earlier, the thing Mickie probably thinks
          I'm clueless about?

Mickie panics. Her head hits the underside of the table with a loud
BANG! Viv pulls her down to the floor and covers her mouth as Mickie
holds her head in exaggerated pain.

Stan and Foz look around a bit and shrug, then head for the front
door.

                         FOZ
          So what's your plan?

                         STAN
          I'm gonna show her who's clueless and do
          something she'll never forget --

They go out the door. As it closes behind them, Mickie jumps up,
racing after them, dragging Viv behind her. She pastes her ear to the
door, trying to hear.

                         VIV
          Can we do something about these handcuffs
          now?

                         MICKIE
          Shhh!

She digs in her pocket and hands Viv a key.

                         VIV
          You had a key this whole time!

                         MICKIE
          One of the perks of owning a Whatever
          shop -- Ahh, they're too far away!

They get out of the handcuffs.

                         MICKIE (CONT'D)
          He knows, Viv! I don't know how --

                         VIV
          Well, he's not Foz . . .

                    MICKIE
     -- and he said he's making a plan -- you
don't suppose . . .

                    VIV
     Oh, Mickie, not Stan!

                    MICKIE
     If only some completely random thing that
     could make me some money would happen!

The door flings open and in leaps THE LOVELY VELMA with huge,
gorgeous blonde hair and a shimmery, sequined gown.

                    VELMA
     Ladies and gentlemen, Mr. Guy St. Guy!

APPLAUSE.

Gameshow host GUY ST. GUY, in a shiny tux, trots in with a mike in
his hand.

                    GUY ST. GUY
     Thank, you, thank you all! And a big hand
     for my charming and always-delightful
     assistant -- the lovely Velma!

More APPLAUSE. Velma curtsies, poses, and blows kisses to the
audience.

                    GUY ST. GUY
                    (To Mickie)
     Are you Mrs. Mickie Puckett --

                    MICKIE
     Yes . . .

                    GUY ST. GUY
      -- of 707 Marshall Avenue --

                    MICKIE
     Yes --

                    GUY ST. GUY
     -- Webster Groves, Missouri --

                    MICKIE
     Yes!

                    GUY ST. GUY
     -- 63119 -- Partario <u>what</u> --

                    MICKIE
     Yes!!

GUY ST. GUY

Then it's time for you to play --

GUY ST. GUY & VELMA
(Together)

Hold That Prize!

MICKIE

It's the show I called in for!

VIV
(Aside)

Didn't see that one comin'!

GUY ST. GUY

All right, Mrs. Puckett, as always, the object of Hold That Prize is for our contestant to answer a series of completely random questions in one minute. For each answer you get right, you're handed a wonderful prize from one of our generous sponsors --

MICKIE

Oh, Yay!!

GUY ST. GUY

-- while for each answer you get wrong you'll be handed a bowling ball!

MICKIE

Oh, yay -- wait, what?

GUY ST. GUY

At the end of one minute, as long as you haven't dropped any bowling balls, whatever prizes you're still holding are yours to keep! Let's get started --

MICKIE

Wait, did you say bowling balls?

GUY ST. GUY

Velma, start the clock. Mickie, what is the name of the Lone Ranger's nephew's horse?

MICKIE

Victor!

DING!

                              MICKIE (CONT'D)
                         (To Viv)
                    And you thought it was silly watching "A
                    Christmas Story" every year!

                              GUY ST. GUY
                    Correct!

Velma hands her a huge bag of money.

                              MICKIE
                    Viv, look!

                              GUY ST. GUY
                    Next question: What is a flying rat?

                              MICKIE
                    A pigeon!

DING!

                              GUY ST. GUY
                    Correct!

Velma hands her a giant gift-wrapped box. Mickie struggles with the
two items.

                              VIV
                    Don't let go of that bag!

                              GUY ST. GUY
                    What is the air speed velocity of an
                    unladen swallow?

                              MICKIE
                    African or European?

                              GUY ST. GUY
                    Doesn't matter!

                              MICKIE
                    I don't know!

BUZZ! Velma lugs over a bowling ball and drops it in Mickie's arms.

                              GUY ST. GUY
                    What is a Jiffy?

                              MICKIE
                    A kind of peanut butter?

BUZZ!

                              GUY ST. GUY
                    Wrong! It's a unit of time equal to one
                    one-hundredth of a second!

Velma lugs over another bowling ball and drops it in Mickie's arms.
Mickie struggles.

> MICKIE
>
> Ooof!

> GUY ST. GUY
>
> What is a pregnant goldfish called?

> MICKIE
>
> Having a fishstick in the oven?

BUZZ!

> GUY ST. GUY
>
> Wrong! It's called a twit!

Velma lugs over another bowling ball. Mickie struggles more.

> MICKIE
>
> Viv, I can't --

> VIV
>
> Yes you can!

> GUY ST. GUY
>
> Who put the Ram in the Ramalamadingdong?

> MICKIE
>
> What does that even mean?

BUZZ!

> GUY ST. GUY
>
> Wrong!

Another bowling ball.

> GUY ST. GUY (CONT'D)
>
> Remember, Mickie, you have to hold on to
> <u>all</u> the bowling balls to keep <u>any</u> prize!

Mickie clutches it all tighter, determined.

> GUY ST. GUY (CONT'D)
>
> Who is Keyser Soze?

> MICKIE
>
> Kevin Spacey!

> GUY ST. GUY
> (Glancing offstage)
> Judges? (Beat)
> (To Mickie)
> We'll allow that!

*DING!* Velma stuffs a glittery dress him Mickie's arms.

                    GUY ST. GUY (CONT'D)
          What did you have for breakfast today?

                    MICKIE
          Special K and yogurt!

BUZZ!

                    GUY ST. GUY
          Wrong! It was a pop-tart and a Diet Coke!

Another bowling ball. Mickie drops the gift box.

                    VIV
          Mickie, be careful!

                    MICKIE
          I'm trying!

                    GUY ST. GUY
          What is the name of the dog on the
          Crackerjack box?

                    MICKIE
          Fido?

BUZZ!

                    GUY ST. GUY
          Wrong! It's Bingo!

One more bowling ball. Mickie struggles, sways back and
forth --

                    MICKIE
          I can do this! Next question!

                    GUY ST. GUY
          Where is --

A bowling ball slips from Mickie's arms. She grabs at it --
-- and drops everything.

DING! DING! DING!

                    GUY ST. GUY (CONT'D)
          And that means we're out of time! Sorry
          Mickie, you were so close, too!

                    MICKIE
          But --

                    GUY ST. GUY
          It's been a pleasure!

                    MICKIE
          -- But I --

Velma gathers up all the prizes and tosses them out the front door.

                    VELMA
          And we thank you for playing!

                    MICKIE
          But I was so close!

                    GUY ST. GUY
          You know, I was a little disappointed for
          you, too --

                    MICKIE
          You weren't the only one. Maybe we can do
          another round --

                    GUY ST. GUY
          -- and then I saw that Crackerjack box over
          there. I won't even insult you by asking
          what you want for it -- I know I can't
          afford it!

                    MICKIE
          -- call this one a mulligan -- what did you
          say?

                    GUY ST. GUY
          Oh, I collect Crackerjack memorabilia --
          that's an 1899 box, still unopened!

Listening, Viv runs to Mickie's computer behind the counter.

                    MICKIE
              (Kind of in shock)
          I guess that means the prize is still
          inside, too . . .

                    GUY ST. GUY
          They hadn't started putting prizes in
          Crackerjack back then.

                    MICKIE
          What do you know about that . . .

                    GUY ST. GUY
          Box like that's worth a fortune. Well, I
          hope you enjoyed the game.
              (To the characters and the audience)
          Good night, everybody!

Velma poses more and blows kisses again, then slinks out behind Guy
St. Guy.

Viv SCREAMS!

> MICKIE
>
> Viv, what is it?

> VIV
>
> The box!

> MICKIE
>
> Yeah?

> VIV
>
> The, the, the one Mr. Shiny-lapels there
> was talking about --

> MICKIE
>
> He said he collects them, but it was too
> expensive -- I couldn't even make <u>that</u>
> sale!

> VIV
>
> Look how much it sells for online!

Mickie leans in and SCREAMS. She and Viv jump up and down hugging.

> MICKIE
>
> That'll cover all the bills!

> VIV
>
> And Stan won't have to do whatever he's
> planning!

> MICKIE
>
> Okay, okay . . . let's go upstairs, get the
> phone numbers for the local newspapers --
> Oh! And the name of that big international
> collector guy that came through here last
> month.

> VIV
>
> The one that was all . . .

> MICKIE
>
> I think all those guys are like that, but
> yeah.

They head through the back door, making plans.

As the back door closes, Foz enters through the front door.

> FOZ
>
> Viv, I can't find our --

He looks around, realizes no one's around.

> FOZ (CONT'D)
> Viv! Viviaaaan! Viiiiiiiv! (Beat) I thought
> I 'eard someone over 'ere . . .

He looks around more, then puts a hand on his stomach.

> FOZ (CONT'D)
> Boy George, am I hungry!

He spots the Crackerjack box.

> FOZ (CONT'D)
> Ooooh, Crackerjack!

Foz opens it, and tries to shake some in his hand. The whole thing slides out in one stuck-together block.

> FOZ (CONT'D)
> Rather like a granola bar, isn't it?

He takes a bite and chews like it's a block of tar. Then he peers into the box.

> FOZ (CONT'D)
> Wot?!? No prize?!? An 'at's the best part!

He shrugs and closes the box back up, putting it back right where he found it. He wanders a bit.

> FOZ (CONT'D)
> Now, wot'd I come over 'ere for in the
> first place? Well, better get back to Stan.

He exits the front door.

END SCENE 2.

SCENE 3:

Mickie and Viv are in the shop with a REPORTER and PHOTOGRAPHER, who are nosing around and setting up. Mickie's so excited she can hardly contain herself.

> VIV
> This is so exciting, Mickie! A reporter and
> a photographer from the newspaper to cover
> your find and turn it into a story!

> MICKIE
> I know!

The Reporter wanders over.

> VIV
> Are you nervous?

                    MICKIE
Oh, yeah.

                    REPORTER
First time?

                    MICKIE
No, I've been nervous before.

                    REPORTER
I'm really glad you gave our newspaper a
heads-up on your story, Mrs. Puckett. This
is exactly the kind of thing people love to
hear about -- it's so "Antiques Roadshow".

                    MICKIE
Well, that's me, just trying to help others
in my community
          (To Viv)
While solving my problems with all the
bills and getting free publicity for the
shop!

The Reporter points to the Crackerjack box, which is in exactly the
same position as it was before (neither the reporter nor the
Photographer have -- or will -- touch it in this scene).

                    REPORTER
So, this box of Crackerjack's actually a
priceless antique?

                    MICKIE
Oh, it has a price.

                    REPORTER
And noted collectibles expert and master
collector Jeff Albertson is coming to take
it off your hands?

                    MICKIE
Oh yes. That's what I've always wanted for
my Whatever shop -- a place where people
can find the things they need and the
things they've wanted but haven't been able
to find.

                    REPORTER
That's a great quote.

                    MICKIE
Why, thank you.

The Photographer's camera flashes.

                    REPORTER
          I tell you what, why don't we move you over
          here, get you next to the box?

                    MICKIE
          Actually, I think the light's better over
          here --

As the Reporter and Photographer turn to do some stage business, she picks up the box and notices how light it is. She opens it --

-- Looks inside --

-- Shakes it --

-- And realizes it's empty with a funny-terrified face.

The Reporter turns back to her. She composes herself instantly, forcing a smile.

                    REPORTER
          Oh, I didn't think you'd want to handle
          something that valuable. But a shot of you
          holding it would be great!

                    PHOTOGRAPHER
                (To Reporter)
          Hey, can you give me a hand with this
          camera, first?

                    REPORTER
          Excuse us.

The two turn away from Mickie and Viv and do some business monkeying with the camera.

                    MICKIE
          Viv -- Viv!

                    VIV
          What?

                    MICKIE
          It's empty!

                    VIV
          What is?

                    MICKIE
          The box!

                    VIV
          What are you talking about? What box?

Mickie turns the Crackerjack box upside-down and shakes it. Viv gasps loudly.

The Reporter and Photographer turn back to them. Mickie and Viv force smiles and wave. The Reporter and Photographer go back to what they were doing.

> MICKIE
> The thing that was going to save me --
> gone!

> VIV
> What are you going to do?

> MICKIE
> I don't know!

> REPORTER
> I think we're ready now Mrs. Puckett.

Mickie and Viv whirl and clench their teeth in fake smiles.

> PHOTOGRAPHER
> I'll do a few whenever you're ready.

Almost in tears, Mickie forces a clenched smile, and after a shot or two, even does a sad thumbs-up.

> PHOTOGRAPHER
> Super. Just what we needed from you. Say,
> would you mind if we wandered around and
> took some pictures?

> MICKIE
> (Still forcing it)
> Sure.

The reporter and photographer start wandering around the set, picking up FRAMED PICTURES setting on the tables and hanging on the walls and carrying them off.

> REPORTER
> We'll be in touch.

They leave.

Mickie sags, looking into the empty box.

> MICKIE
> What are we going to do? That collector
> will be here the day after tomorrow!

> VIV
> I don't know.

                    MICKIE
Oh Viv, I'm freaking out. I don't know what
to do now! Everything's going to be all
right, isn't it?

Viv looks like she's about to nod "yes."

                    VIV
No.

                                    END SCENE 3.

                                    END ACT ONE.

ACT TWO


SCENE 1:

Mickie's pacing anxiously in the shop as Viv taps her foot, thinking hard.

>                    MICKIE
>          Who'd be a big enough boob to eat hundred-
>          year-old box of crackerjack?

>                    VIV
>               (Eyes suddenly wide)
>          Foz! Oh, I'm sorry, Mickie.

Stan comes in, reading a NEWSPAPER.

>                    STAN
>          Well, the review for our gig the other
>          night ran today.

Mickie's too down, so Viv jumps in to cover for her.

>                    VIV
>          So, what'd they say?

>                    STAN
>          They didn't say anything.

>                    VIV
>          You just told me the review ran.

>                    STAN
>          It did, but all they put in was a picture.

He hands her the paper. Curious, Mickie looks over Viv's shoulder.

>                    MICKIE
>          Why is that dog in the photo squatting like
>          that -- oh. Oh!

>                    VIV
>          Oh, my!

Foz enters.

>                    VIV (CONT'D)
>          I'm sorry, Stan. That's a terrible review.

She hands the newspaper off to Mickie.

>                    MICKIE
>          And more bad news -- look -- that swine flu
>          thing's getting worse.

She hands the paper to Foz.

                         FOZ
          Ooh! There's a sale at Penney's!

Viv snatches the paper away from him.

                         STAN
          I'm gonna go upstairs. I didn't sleep well
          last night.

                         MICKIE
          You were pretty restless. Why don't you
          take a nap?

                         STAN
          Best idea I've heard today.

Stan heads for the back door and exits.

                         VIV
          You think we --

A ROOSTER CROWS. Mickie and Viv react, Viv dropping the newspaper.
Foz picks it up and starts reading, oblivious.

Stan re-enters immediately.

                         STAN
          <u>Why</u> is there a rooster in our kitchen? And
          why did it <u>crow</u> when I turned on the light?

Lulu runs in from the back, in a flurry of chicken feathers.

                         LULU
          Uh, <u>hi</u> daddy!

                         STAN
          Lulu, why do I think this has something to
          do with science fair?

                         LULU
          It's my new project. I'm trying to see if I
          can condition a rooster to crow any time a
          light comes on.

                         STAN
          Because . . .?

                         LULU
           . . . because I couldn't do the electro-
          shock thing with Partario.

                         STAN
          What happened to butterfly collections and
          baking soda volcanoes?

                         STAN (CONT'D)
          Or bread mold? Everyone used to do bread
          mold when I was a kid.

                         LULU
          Those weren't . . . scien<u>tastic</u> enough.

                         STAN
          Whatever.

He goes through the back door again.

The ROOSTER CROWS.

                         VIV
          Foz, look at the time.

He looks up, surprised.

                         FOZ
          Oh, right.

He walks out the front.

                         MICKIE
          What's he late for?

                         VIV
          Nothing. I just wanted to talk to you alone
          for a minute.

                         MICKIE
          Is it always that easy?

                         VIV
          Usually easier. (Beat) So, after yesterday,
          with the box . . .

                         MICKIE
          Yeah . . .

                         VIV
          What are you going to do?

                         MICKIE
          I worked on it last night.

                         VIV
          Calling back that Albertson guy?

                         MICKIE
          No, figuring out a way I can still sell him
          the box.

She goes behind the counter and produces the Crackerjack box. She
hands it to Viv.

Viv pops open the top immediately.

                    VIV
          Oh, the scotch tape loops holding it closed
          don't seem to be working so well.
                    (Sarcastic)
          I'm surprised you didn't just wrap it in
          duct tape.

                    MICKIE
          I was out.

Viv peers inside the box.

                    VIV
          What do you have in here? (Beat) This is
          cheese popcorn!

                    MICKIE
          It's all I had in the house last night.

Viv sniffs it.

                    VIV (CONT'D)
          Mixed with maple syrup?!?

                    MICKIE
          I panicked, okay? Tried to fix it with what
          I had on hand. If I can just come up with
          an idea --

                    VIV
          I got an idea: Why don't we not go with
          your idea and go with the "Tell Stan" idea?

                    MICKIE
          Not yet, Viv. I know I can fix all this if
          I can just think of something.

Elvira enters.

                    ELVIRA
          P-M-F-I, M-D, G-A-S?

Viv's angling to look out the window.

                    VIV
                    (Distracted)
          Sure, sweetheart . . .

                    ELVIRA
          B-I-F --

                    VIV
          Hang on -- Did you see your father outside?

                    ELVIRA
          N-O-

                    VIV
          He must've turned the wrong way.

                    MICKIE
          You live next door.

                    VIV
          You'd thing that would give him at least a
          fifty-fifty shot. Elvira, come on, we
          better go find him.

Viv heads for the door. Elvira falls in behind her.

                    ELVIRA
          A-D-I-P!

They exit. Mickie paces, clearly worried.

                    PARTARIO (OS)
          Mom! I've got the mail! And there's a
          package!

Partario staggers in the front door, barely holding up a HUGE
REFRIGERATOR-SIZED BOX and clutching a couple of ENVELOPES in one
hand.

                    MICKIE
                 (Without turning)
          What is it, Partario?

Partario tries to angle his head back enough to read the heavy box.

                    PARTARIO
          I can't see it.

                    MICKIE
          What do you mean you can't -- oh, Partario,
          you shouldn't have carried that up the
          front steps yourself! Here let me get that.

She crosses over to him and takes the two envelopes from his hand.
Partario staggers backwards out the door as she opens one envelope,
then he staggers back in.

                    MICKIE (CONT'D)
                 (Without turning)
          One more bill I can add to the stack I
          can't do anything about.

                    PARTARIO
          Uh, Mom?

                         MICKIE
          Yes, dear?

                         PARTARIO
          Where do you want this?

                         MICKIE
          Oh, just put it down --

Partario starts to lower it to the floor, huffing and grunting.

                         MICKIE (CONT'D)
          -- over in the corner there.

Partario hefts it back up and wobbles with it toward the corner.

Mickie looks at the next envelope.

                         MICKIE (CONT'D)
          A letter from my old high school?

She opens the letter as Partario reaches the corner

                         MICKIE (CONT'D)
          Oh, Partario, not there. In the front, by
          the window.

Partario looks from her to the window and back again with an "are you
kidding me?" look, then shifts back and forth to turn around and head
back.

                         MICKIE (CONT'D)
                    (Reading)
          . . . twenty-second reunion of the class
          of . . . who does a twenty-second
          anniversary reunion? (Beat) What? "to
          celebrate the enormous successes of our
          former class president, successful CEO
          Leslie Duddy and raise funds for her run
          for US Senator?" Gimme a break!

Partario barely makes it to the front, sinking lower with each step.
As he's about to put it down --

                         MICKIE
                    (Absently)
          Partario, right here, by the desk . . .

She goes back to the letter. Partario huffs and lurches toward his
mother, tottering --

 -- teetering --

 -- until he sets it down right next to her.

                              MICKIE
          Oh, good, you found someplace to put it.
          Did you get your lunchbox washed out from
          today yet?

                              PARTARIO
          No.

                              MICKIE
          Why not?

                              PARTARIO
          'cuz I don't have it.

                              MICKIE
          Did you leave it at school again.

                              PARTARIO
          No . . . (Beat) I lost it.

                              MICKIE
          Partario! That's the third one since school
          started this year! I'm not going to keep
          getting you new ones.

                              PARTARIO
          But I need one to bring my lunch!

      She squints at the label on the box.

                              MICKIE
          Oh, great. Well, lucky for you this came
          in.

                              PARTARIO
          What is it?

                              MICKIE
          A collection of lunchboxes I picked up
          cheap at an auction. I thought some parents
          might see them in the window and be drawn
          into the shop.

                              PARTARIO
          I don't want an <u>old</u> lunchbox!

                              MICKIE
          They're called <u>vintage</u> in this business.
          Open the box and pick one out.

      Partario tips over the box and crawls in. He sticks his head out.

                              PARTARIO
          I don't know what <u>any</u> of these are <u>from</u>.

                    MICKIE
          Don't care.

                    PARTARIO
          My friends will make fun of me!

                    MICKIE
          How bad can it be?

He crawls back inside the box. The box shakes crazily as he roots
around before sticking his head back out.

                    PARTARIO
          Like this one: What does "Dy-no-mite!"
          mean?
                    (Looks at another)
          Who's "That Girl"?
                    (And another)
          And what's a <u>flying</u> <u>nun</u>?

                    MICKIE
          Whatever, Partario, just pick one.

Lulu enters.

                    LULU
          Baby bro playing in the big box?

                    PARTARIO
          I'm not playing in the box! (Beat) Hey,
          Mom, can I keep this box?

Mickie's looking at the bill in her hands.

                    MICKIE
          Oh, what am I going to do?

                    LULU
          About what, Mom?

                    MICKIE
          Nothing you need to worry about. I'm going
          to have to tough it out, cowgirl up,
          soldier on, and do my duty!

Partario snickers.

                    MICKIE (CONT'D)
          What?

Partario can't contain himself any more.

                    PARTARIO
                    (Laughing)
          You said "doodie".

> MICKIE
> I said "duty."

He laughs more.

> MICKIE (CONT'D)
> Like a responsibility. Like "I have to do
> my duty."

Partario roars with laughter.

> PARTARIO
> You said you have to do your doodie!

> MICKIE
> Partario, knock it off! You're gonna make
> me crotchety!!

Lulu starts laughing.

> MICKIE (CONT'D)
> (To Lulu)
> What?!?

> LULU
> Crotchety!

Both kids laugh. Mickie's exasperated.

> LULU (CONT'D)
> Hey Mom, can I go over to Elvira's?

> MICKIE
> Sure. Be home before dinner.

> LULU
> 'kay.

Lulu exits.

BANG! The front door flies open. With a peg leg and wearing an old-fashioned white nurse's dress and hat, NURSE AHAB limps in, bent over, her face all scrunched up.

> PARTARIO
> Mom, it's the new school nurse -- run!

Mickie grabs him by the collar as he tries to take off, and he runs in place comically for a beat.

Nurse Ahab leads in several SWINE FLU PATIENTS all in hospital gowns, coughing and oinking. She starts arranging them in the shop.

> NURSE AHAB
> Arrh, it's the swine flu! The swine flu!

                         MICKIE
          I'm sorry, this may be a whatever shop, but
          it's not a clinic!

                         NURSE AHAB
          Arrrh, it be one now!

                         MICKIE
          You can't --

                         NURSE AHAB
          Aye, I can. Under article five, section
          sixty-three of the PTO parents code, I can
          commandeer any space belongin' to a PTO
          parent within a quarter mile of Avery for
          the clinic when the one at school be
          full -- and it be!

                         MICKIE
                  (Pleasant, like a suggestion)
          Partario, run.

He takes off.

                         MICKIE (CONT'D)
                  (Calling after him)
          Go in the back room -- you'll be safe --

He dashes through the door. As it closes behind him, there's a loud
CRASH of stuff falling.

                         PARTARIO (OS)
          Owww!

Mickie starts to look concerned --

 -- the ROOSTER CROWS --

-- and Mickie gives up.

                         MICKIE
          Whatever.
                  (To Nurse Ahab)
          What am I supposed to do with all these
          sick people?

                         NURSE AHAB
          For the most part, just leave 'em be. Ye
          can bring 'em a drinka water every hour or
          so. But all they really do is lay there and
          cough.

One of the Swine Flu Patients oinks.

                    NURSE AHAB (CONT'D)
          And oink on occasion --

A couple more start coughing and oinking.

                    NURSE AHAB (CONT'D)
          -- Constantly.

                    MICKIE
          Well, it's just -- you see, my background's
          in graphic design -- although I did some
          theatre work and probably should volunteer
          for the Avery Play some time (Beat) -- but
          I don't know anything about medicine.

The coughing and oinking increases. Nurse Ahab claps her hands to her
ears.

                    NURSE AHAB
          Oh, the oinkin'! The oinkin'!

                    MICKIE
          I can see how that would get on your --

                    NURSE AHAB
          I can't stand it! Not again! It's like
          Burma back in twenty-nine!

                    MICKIE
          Nineteen twenty-nine?

                    NURSE AHAB
          Oh, they thought they had me then, the sly,
          piggy little bugs! The oinkin'! The
          oinkin'!

                    MICKIE
          Maybe I can get you a chair?

Mickie steps away and grabs a chair as Nurse Ahab begins pacing.

                    NURSE AHAB
          The oinkin'! The oinkin'!

Mickie comes back with the chair, and staring, stunned, at Nurse
Ahab, she sits down on it herself and leans forward to watch.

                    NURSE AHAB (CONT'D)
          I can't stand it any more! I can't stand
          it!

She heads for the door.

> MICKIE
> Wait! What am I supposed to do? Is there
> anything I should worry about?

> NURSE AHAB
> Only if it gets dark! An' they get quiet-
> like all at once!

She exits, and the coughing and oinking subsides.

Mickie wanders back to center stage, tiptoeing, not wanting to touch anything, the occasional cough and oink startling her.

> MICKIE
> I guess this isn't too bad . . .

The room goes dark.

> MICKIE (CONT'D)
> Wow, it gets dark quickly this time of
> year.

The coughing and oinking stops.

> MICKIE (CONT'D)
> At least they've all stopped with the
> coughing and oinking.

Behind her, the Swine Flu Patients, now all with PIG SNOUTS, shamble to their feet and stalk toward the front of the stage, slow, shuffling, like the undead.

> MICKIE (CONT'D)
> Hold on, that nurse just said something
> about this --

The Swine Flu Patients shuffle up to her. She startles --

-- And they go right past her, taking up positions center stage as she backs away, watching.

MUSICAL NUMBER:

A dance performance to "Thriller" with Nurse Ahab re-joining the Swine Flu Patients

Wrapping up their dance, the Swine Flu Patients amble out the front door. In a GAS MASK behind them, Mickie shoos them out, spraying after then from a huge BUG-SPRAY TANK labeled LYSOL.

Mickie sighs.

                    MICKIE
        Whatever!

                                      END SCENE 1.

SCENE 2:

Foz enters.

                    MICKIE
        Hey Foz! Did Viv and Elvira ever find you?

                    FOZ
        Who?

                    MICKIE
        Your wife and daughter?

He shakes his head like she's speaking a foreign language.

                    MICKIE (CONT'D)
        The tall one and the little one that live
        in your house?

                    FOZ
        Riiiiiiight . . . .

                    MICKIE
        They were --

                    FOZ
        . . . Riiiiiiight . . . .'aven't seen
        either of 'em all day.

He spots an ACTION FIGURE on the shelf.

                    FOZ (CONT'D)
        Oh, now <u>this</u> is <u>brilliant</u>!

                    MICKIE
        What?

                    FOZ
        This is a Captain Radar Missile Man action
        figure! Used to 'ave one when I was a lad!

                    MICKIE
         (Aside)
        <u>That</u> he remembers.
         (To Foz)
        Tell ya what, just take it, have fun with
        it.

                              FOZ
                Thank you, luv! Very kind o' you.

He exits, passing Viv as she enters.

                              VIV
                    (Over her shoulder to Foz)
                I'll be home in just a bit! Hey, Mickie!

                              MICKIE
                Hi.

                              VIV
                Where's Stan?

                              MICKIE
                I think he's in the back, spankin' the --

A PIERCING CHIMP SCREECH cuts her off.

Stan backs in through the back door, jabbing a BANANA at something
off stage

                              STAN
                And don't climb in the cabinet like that
                again! Next time you want a banana, you ask
                first!

He turns around, waving the banana angrily.

                              STAN (CONT'D)
                Mickie, that monkey was one of the worst
                pet ideas we ever let the kids talk us
                into!

                              VIV
                    (To Mickie)
                If you sold it . . .

                              MICKIE
                Nahh.

                              STAN
                Okay, honey, I'm gonna head out. You've got
                plans for tonight, right, so the babysitter
                will be here when one of us gets home?

                              MICKIE
                Val should be here any minute.

                              STAN
                Cool. Then I'll see you later.

                              MICKIE
                Bye.

He exits.

                    MICKIE (CONT'D)
          Viv, I've got one more idea.

                    VIV
          Can we codename this plan "The Ninny Plan"?

                    MICKIE
          This one's got a good shot at working. But
          I need help.

                    VIV
          (Beat) All right, I'm in. What is it?

Viv's cell phone rings.

                    VIV (CONT'D)
          Oh, that's my phone.

She pulls out her cell phone and answers it.

                    VIV (CONT'D)
              (Like she's talking to a toddler)
          Hi honey. No, I'll be a little while
          yet . . . I'm talking with Mrs. Puckett.
          (Beat) I can tuck you in when I get home.
          (Beat) No, I think you've watched enough TV
          tonight and you need to get to bed now.
          (Beat) You can look at a book. Yes, you
          have to brush your teeth tonight. (Beat)
          No, I don't know where your jammies with
          the hearts are. You just get to bed now,
          okay. I better find you there when I get
          home. No, you don't have to be asleep --
          you can say good night to me. (Beat) Uh
          huh. Okay. Love you too, honey.

She hangs up.

                    VIV (CONT'D)
          That was Foz. I better stop by the house
          before we go.

                    MICKIE
          Y'know, if it'd be easier, one more kid
          won't be a problem for the babysitter, if
          you want to have Elvira come over here.

                    VIV
          No, no -- I need her home to mind Foz.

                    MICKIE
          Oh, right, after that whole thing with the
          oven. Did you ever get rid of the wet llama
          smell?

Viv shakes her head.

The babysitter, VAL, enters, a 16 year-old from Webster High School
dressed in the height of fashion -- for 1985.

                    VAL
          Like, Hello Mrs. P.

                    MICKIE
          Hi, Val. Thanks for coming on such short
          notice.

                    VAL
          Totally! Like, I can way use the extra
          cash!

Viv looks confused.

                    VIV
                (To Mickie)
          Isn't she about 25 years behind --

                    MICKIE
          I don't even try to figure it out any more.
                (To Val)
          Glad to help out there. How's that
          boyfriend of yours?

                    VAL
          Skip? Gag me with a spoon! We're like so
          totally over!

                    MICKIE
          Oh, I didn't mean to --

                    VAL
          -- cause we were like, talking about music
          and he said he didn't like Chris DeBurgh
          and I was like, uh, hello, "Lady in Red"
          what's your damage? And he was all "Not
          even" and I was all "Even" and he goes "Not
          even" --

                    MICKIE
          Val, we're running late.

                    VAL
          Oh, fer sure.

>                    MICKIE
>     Lulu and Partario are upstairs. They're
>     supposed to be changing for bed, and they
>     know you're watching them tonight.

>                    VAL
>     No problemo!

>                    MICKIE
>     And you have my cell number.

>                    VAL
>     Totally. Oh, just to okay it with you, I
>     have this absolutely heinous literature
>     test tomorrow, and my friend Heather and I
>     were going to study together, and I wanted
>     to make sure it's completely tubular with
>     you that she come over while I'm sitting
>     your kids --

>                    MICKIE
>     Not a problem. We just have to go.

>                    VAL
>     'kay!

Val puts on a pair of Walkman-style headphones and starts bobbing her head like she's listening to some tune. Viv squints at her.

>                    VIV
>               (To Mickie)
>     You know her headphones aren't plugged in
>     to anything?

>                    MICKIE
>     She does that.

Mickie and Viv exit.

Val sits for a bit, bobbing her head, when HEATHER, also in 80s gear, enters.

>                    HEATHER
>     Like, sorry I'm so totally late.

>                    VAL
>     Are you all right? You look all out of
>     breath!

>                    HEATHER
>     I was getting my car looked at!

                    VAL
Omigawsh, the awesome new pink one your
parents gave you for your birthday --

                    HEATHER
Yah --

                    VAL
What happened to it?

                    HEATHER
You won't believe it! When I was coming
home from the mall the other day, I was
totally caught in that gnarly hail we had,
and my car was pelted like grody elves with
hammers had gone after it!

                    VAL
Omigawsh!

Val runs to the window to see and gasps.

                    VAL (CONT'D)
Omigawsh!

                    HEATHER
So I took it to the body place, on my way
over here and the guy working there -- not
the creepy old one that's, like, you know,
more ancient than my dad --

                    VAL
Barf!

                    HEATHER & VAL
Gag me with a spoon <u>fer</u> <u>sher</u>!

                    HEATHER
But the other guy there, the cute one that
looks like he could <u>totally</u> go to Webster
University but he's probably going to tech
school and that's why he's working in a
body shop --

                    VAL
Totally!

                    HEATHER
-- like, he told me all I had to do was
crouch down behind the car and blow hard in
the tailpipe to make the dents all pop out
again.

>                         VAL
>           Uh, and what did you do after he told you
>           that?

>                         HEATHER
>           I tried for like an hour, and it <u>didn't</u>
>           <u>work</u>!

>                         VAL
>           Well, <u>duh</u>!

>                         HEATHER
>           What do you mean "duh"?

>                         VAL
>                    (Points to the car )
>           Like, <u>helloooo</u>! You need to <u>roll</u> <u>up</u> all the
>           <u>windows</u> first!

>                         HEATHER
>           Oh, <u>mega</u>-duh!

>                         VAL
>           I'm just glad you weren't in that bogus
>           disaster at the mall!

>                         HEATHER
>           No way! What happened?

>                         VAL
>           Brittany called me from the mall -- she was
>           one of the ones trapped!

>                         HEATHER
>           Omigawsh!

>                         VAL
>           The power went out, and Brittany and, like,
>           a whole bunch of our friends were totally
>           stuck on the <u>escalator</u> for like, <u>hours</u>!

>                         HEATHER
>           Omigawsh!

>                         VAL
>           Omigawsh!

Mickie and Viv enter wearing GRASS SKIRTS and COCONUT BRAS (over
their regular clothes, of course). Mickie has a bunch of BALLOONS,
while Viv's carrying a TOASTER. Both look dejected.

>                         VIV
>           I thought for sure that was going to work.

                    MICKIE
          Me too. Where do you think it went wrong?

                    VIV
          I don't think we had enough muffin pans.

                    MICKIE
          And if we'd brought a ladder --

                    VIV
                (Nodding)
          Or at least a step-stool.

                    MICKIE
          Twenty-twenty hindsight, right? What am I
          going to do

Toast pops out of Viv's toaster.

                    VIV
          Toast?

Mickie waves it off.

                    MICKIE
          Thanks, Val.
                (Realizes she has no money on her)
          Mind if I pay you this weekend?

Val looks like she minds, rolling her eyes and huffing.

                    VAL
          No problemo, Mrs. P.

Heather and Val gather their things.

                    VAL (CONT'D)
          You can give it to my mom for me when you
          see her at the PTO. Later!

She and Heather exit.

                    MICKIE
          Look at the time! Viv, we better run and
          change before Stan and Foz get back.

They go in the back.

The ROOSTER CROWS.

Stan and Foz peek in the front door.

                    STAN
          Good! Looks like no one's around!

                    FOZ
          You smell coconut?

Stan waves him off, listening, worried they'll be caught.

                    FOZ (CONT'D)
          Why in the name of Keith Richards are we
          sneakin' around like this?

                    STAN
          So we can get the decorations up for
          Mickie's fortieth birthday surprise.

DRAMATIC CUE SOUND: *Dun-Dun-Duuuuun!*

Foz looks around for where the music's coming from.

The two walk in, Stan with an armful of rolled up posters/banners, Foz with a BOX OF BOWLING BALLS.

Stan does a double-take at the box.

                    STAN
          Where did you get <u>bowling</u> <u>balls</u>? We didn't
          have those when we left your house.

Foz scoots up right behind Stan.

                    FOZ
          Found 'em in the bushes by your front
          steps.

                    STAN
          Whatever.

                    FOZ
          Hey, 'at's what Mickie always says!

                    STAN
          Shhh! We don't need to call any attention
          to ourselves. Back up a bit --

He nudges Foz back a bit. Foz drops the box of bowling balls on Stan's foot.

                    STAN (CONT'D)
          Oww!

Stan covers his own mouth.

                    FOZ
          Sorry, squire.

Foz picks up the box.

                    STAN
          Just keep the noise down. And back up a
          bit.

He nudges Foz back a bit. Foz drops the box on Stan's foot again.

                         STAN (CONT'D)
          Oww!

Stan covers his own mouth.

                         FOZ
          Sorry, squire.

Foz picks up the box again.

                         STAN
          What are you doing? Be careful with that
          thing! And back up a bit.

He nudges Foz back a bit. Foz drops the box on Stan's foot a third
time.

                         STAN (CONT'D)
          Oww!

Stan covers his own mouth.

                         FOZ
          Sorry, squire.

Foz picks up the box a third time.

                         STAN
          Foz, what do you even have those for?

                         FOZ
          Dunno. Thought they might come in handy.
          Good for a laugh, I suppose.

Stan grabs the box away from him and tosses it out the front door.

                         MICKIE (OS)
          Viv, I think I heard the guys out front!

                         STAN
          Hide!

Foz and Stan duck one way, then another, then grab a couple of
LAMPSHADES off a shelf and put them over their heads, covering their
faces as they stand straight and still.

Mickie and Viv enter.

                         VIV
          Where are they?

                         MICKIE
          I thought for sure I heard someone up here.
          Maybe it was the kids watching TV.

                         VIV
          It's so dark in here.

She walks over to Foz and reaches under his shade.

                    FOZ
          Click!

His shade lights up.

Viv goes back to Mickie.

                    MICKIE
          Maybe Stan won't <u>really</u> go through with
          what he's planning.

                    VIV
          Mickie, I wouldn't worry.

                    MICKIE
          Oh, sure -- he's not going to ruin <u>your</u>
          life with some awful plan!

Stan lifts his lampshade.

                    STAN
                (To Foz)
          How can she know what I'm planning?

Foz lifts his lampshade.

                    FOZ
          Viv always seems to know about things goin'
          on that I don't.

                    STAN
          Foz, that coat rack knows more about what's
          going on than you do.

                    FOZ
          Really? How much for the coat rack, then?

                    STAN
          Shhh!

They quickly get under their lampshades again.

                    VIV
          You don't know he's going to ruin anything.

                    STAN
          And why does she think my plan's going to
          be so awful?

                    MICKIE
          Big day like tomorrow, if things don't go
          exactly right . . . I'm nervous, Viv.

                        STAN
          We gotta get out of here, get to work on
          something <u>new</u>.

                        FOZ
          But they'll see us.

                        STAN
          We need a distraction.

                        FOZ
          I've got ya covered, squire!

Foz steps forward and points out at the audience.

                        FOZ (CONT'D)
          Look! Random dancing!

DANCE MUSIC ("Everybody Dance Now") comes up, and out in the aisles,
some of the moms and dads from the dance numbers are shakin' glow
sticks and their groove thangs.

Mickie and Viv look out in the audience, confused, while Stan and Foz
dash out the door.


                                              END SCENE 2.


SCENE 3

Mickie's in the shop, pacing. On one of the shelves behind her, the
LUNCHBOXES are all lined up.

                        MICKIE
          Haven't been able to figure anything
          out . . . nothing . . . There must be
          <u>something</u> I can do to straighten this all
          <u>out</u> . . .

Viv enters.

                        VIV
          So, what'd he say?

                        MICKIE
          Who?

                        VIV
          The collector guy, Jeff whats-his-face.

Mickie looks away.

                        VIV (CONT"D)
          You called him, right? (Beat) You didn't
          call him?!?

                    MICKIE
     I was up all night --

                    VIV
     Yeah, those weird people dancing outside
     last night creeped me out, too.

                    MICKIE
     No! Trying to <u>think</u> of something. And then
     I nodded off, and when I woke up this
     morning I realized his flight had already
     landed and he was here in town. Maybe he'll
     just take the empty box!

She picks it up off a shelf.

                    MICKIE (CONT'D)
     I wiped out all the popcorn cheese and the
     syrup! The tape pulled away clean -- as
     hundred-year-old boxes go, it's in great
     shape. Maybe he'll give me <u>something</u> for
     it!

                    VIV
     Or maybe when the unopened box he flew
     half-way across the country for turns out
     to be open and empty, he'll <u>get</u> <u>mad</u> <u>and</u>
     <u>leave</u>!

                    MICKIE
     There's the sunshine I always count on you
     for!

                    VIV
     Mickie, you wouldn't even be in all this
     trouble if you'd told Stan <u>everything</u> up
     front!

                    MICKIE
     And I should've phoned the collector when I
     found the box empty and called everything
     off. But now it's too late, so unless
     something miraculous happens . . .

Elvira and Lulu enter, running through the back door.

                    ELVIRA
     O-M-G! O--M--G!!

                    VIV
     What is it, Elvira?

                              ELVIRA
              N-O A-F-J --

Viv sorts through her cards trying to understand what she's saying.

                              VIV
              Wait sweetheart, you're going too fast --
              Uh, P-I—T-R . . . A-F-Z?

                              LULU
              I got this one. Mom -- we were on that
              guy's website --

                              MICKIE
              Yeah --

                              LULU
              Collectorofallthingscolliectible dot com.

                              MICKIE
              Been there --

                              LULU
              Right, but he's got a want list up of the
              things he's looking for and we saw
              something from our store there!

                              MICKIE
              You mean besides the Crackerjack box?

                              LULU
              It's worth more than the Crackerjack box!

                              MICKIE
                      (To Viv)
              I never thought to check anything else on
              his list.
                      (To Lulu)
              What is it, sweetie?

                              LULU
              A toy, one of those, those action figure
              things like Partario used to play with.
              This one's super-rare, and his website says
              there are almost none in existence any
              more -- I'm so nervous I can't think of the
              name of it -- Radar Man ? --

                              MICKIE
              Captain Radar Missile Men!

                              LULU
              Yes! How do you know?

                         MICKIE
              Foz was telling me all about it (Beat as it
              sinks in) -- right before I gave it to him!

In a huge tangle, they all scramble for the door.

SOUND EFFECTS: BOOM!

There's an explosion outside.

                         MICKIE (CONT'D)
              What --

                         ELVIRA
              W-T --!

She clamps a hand over her mouth, caught.

                         VIV
              Elvira Patella Fozzard!

They all stop, confused.

                         MICKIE
                    (Pained)
              Lulu, the website didn't mention why those
              toys are so rare, did it?

                         LULU
              Yeah. It said the missile men had built-in
              firecrackers and were made to blow up.

Foz and Partario enter, laughing and back-slapping.

                         PARTARIO
              That was beastly awesome, Mr. Fozzard.

                         FOZ
              Jus' like when I was a lad -- Boom! By
              Alice Cooper, I used to love watching those
              explode.

Mickie sinks.

                         VIV
              Kids, why don't you all go next door with
              Mr. Fozzard.

They all start to exit. Foz turns back.

                         FOZ
                    (To Viv, indicating Mickie)
              She all right?

                         VIV
              She will be. We'll figure it out. You take
              the kids next door, okay.

                         FOZ
          Right.

Foz and the kids exit.

                         VIV
          So what do we do now?

Mickie composes herself.

                         MICKIE
          I sell him an empty box. People buy those.
          It won't get us as much as I thought, but
          maybe it'll be enough to help out.

                         VIV
          Especially if you tell Stan.

Mickie nods.

                         VIV (CONT'D)
          Sounds like a good plan to me. What time's
          your buyer supposed to get here?

                         MICKIE
          Any time now.

The front door opens and JEFF ALBERTSON, collector of all things
collectible, enters. A John Lovitz-type with thick coke-bottle
glasses on his face, he's wearing sandals, socks, cargo shorts, a
Marvel Comics T-shirt and a suit coat.

                         JEFF ALBERTSON
          Hello. I'm Jeff Albertson, collector. I
          have an appointment with Mickie Puckett?

                         MICKIE
          That's me. Nice to meet you.

                         JEFF ALBERTSON
          Good to meet you. I don't mean to sound
          like I'm in a hurry, but I _am_.

                         MICKIE
          Oh, sure. I have it right over here . . .

Much like the scene with the Reporter & Photographer, Mickie's
_comically_ trying not to cry.

                         MICKIE (CONT'D)
          I do need to tell you, though, there's been
          a _change_ --

                         JEFF ALBERTSON
          Oh?

Jeff Albertson wanders the shop as she talks.

                    MICKIE
          So maybe I can throw something else in for
          you with it -- a lampshade, maybe some
          herbal tea I hear is good for swine flu --
          kind of as a bonus and to make up for --

                    JEFF ALBERTSON
          Thanks, but I have a whole lot of
          everything, so the box is really <u>all</u> I
          <u>need</u>.

                    MICKIE
          O-<u>kay</u> . . .

She heads for the counter where the empty Crackerjack box is.

Jeff drifts past the Lunchboxes and does a double-take. He picks up
one and looks like he's about to have a heart attack. He yanks a
handkerchief from his pocket and mops his face.

                    JEFF ALBERTSON
          This is a, uh, very interesting lunchbox
          you have here.

                    MICKIE
          It's my son's. I have to keep a lot of them
          because he keeps losing them at school.

Jeff claps a hand to his chest. Mickie doesn't notice.

                    JEFF ALBERTSON
          Would you be interested in selling it?

                    MICKIE
                (Like he's kidding her)
          Oh, what would Partario bring his lunch to
          school in?

                    JEFF ALBERTSON
          In his shoes, for all I care. Five
          thousand!

                    MICKIE
          Excuse me?

                    JEFF ALBERTSON
          Okay, ten!

                    MICKIE
          For <u>that</u>?

                    JEFF ALBERTSON
          Twelve!

He takes a slip of paper from his pocket, writes on it, and hands it to Mickie.

> JEFF ALBERTSON (CONT'D)
> My final offer.

Not getting it, she doesn't even look at the paper.

> MICKIE
> But I have your Crackerjack box right over here.

> JEFF ALBERTSON
> You're a shrewd one, Mrs. Puckett, luring me here with that paltry 1899 box of Crackerjack and then leaving a real prize like this for me to just --

> JEFF ALBERTSON (CONT'D)
> (Does "air quotes" with his fingers)
> -- stumble across.
> (Admiring)
> A 1968 "Flying Nun" lunchbox, first edition with side-panel error! I've been trying to lay my hands on one of these for years --

> MICKIE
> I know it's not exactly as I described on the phone --

> JEFF ALBERTSON
> -- But I've lost out on the last three that came on the market to that comic-shop-owning half-wit in Springfield! I don't know why he needs every one that surfaces! I must have this!

> MICKIE
> Okay . . . do you have a price in mind?

He points to the paper in her fingers.

> MICKIE (CONT'D)
> Oh, right.
> (Looks at it)
> That's not much at all. I mean, how many cents is that with all the zeroes in front of it?

He reaches over and turns the paper around so it's right-side-up in her hands.

Mickie reads it and screams. Viv runs to her side.

                JEFF ALBERTSON
      All right, I know, I know, I shouldn't have
      even tried that on you.

He leans in with the pen and adds two zeroes to the end of the number.

Mickie screams again. She shows it to Viv, and she screams.

                MICKIE
      You, you mean this much <u>dollars</u>?

                JEFF ALBERTSON
      I could do it in vintage "Star Wars" action
      figures . . .

                MICKIE
      No, cash is fine.

                JEFF ALBERTSON
      I'll go get it from the car.

He exits.

                MICKIE
      Viv! Did you <u>see</u> that?!?

                VIV
      Yes!

                MICKIE
      I did it! It's enough so I can cover the
      bills, and get the shop in the black for a
      <u>long</u> <u>time</u>!

Stan, Foz, the kids (except Partario), and the rest of the cast enter.

                STAN
      Mickie, on a big day like today, you
      deserve something special!


MUSICAL NUMBER:

A dance performance to "Hey Mickey!"


Partario jumps forward in a cheerleader costume.

                    PARTARIO
        Now I know what I'm doing for Razzmatazz!

                    MICKIE
        Stan, this is so great of you. But how did
        you know?

                    STAN
        How could I not?

                    MICKIE
        I mean, with the Crackerjack box and then
        not the Crackerjack box, and the clown
        suits and the grass skirts and balloons,
        and then the lunchbox thing -- I didn't
        even know about that until it happened!

                    STAN
        I have no idea what you're talking about.

                    MICKIE
        What's all this for?

                    STAN
        Your fortieth birthday!

DRAMATIC CUE SOUND: *Dun-Dun-Duuuuun!*

                    MICKIE
        My what?

                    STAN
        I wanted to do something special for you.

                    MICKIE
        Stan, what's this?

She points at his shirt, in the middle of his chest.

                    STAN
        What?

He looks down.

She flips her hand up and smacks him on the head.

                    STAN
        Oww! What was that for?

                    MICKIE
        For puttin' me through all that!

                    STAN
        All what? It's for your birthday!

                    MICKIE
         My birthday was <u>last</u> <u>week</u>!

                     FOZ
                   (Aside)
         Didn't see 'at one comin'!

Mickie group hugs Stan, Viv, Foz, and the kids.

                    MICKIE
         Oh, whatever!


                                        END SCENE 3.

                                        END ACT TWO.

                                        CURTAIN.


                    <u>THE END</u>

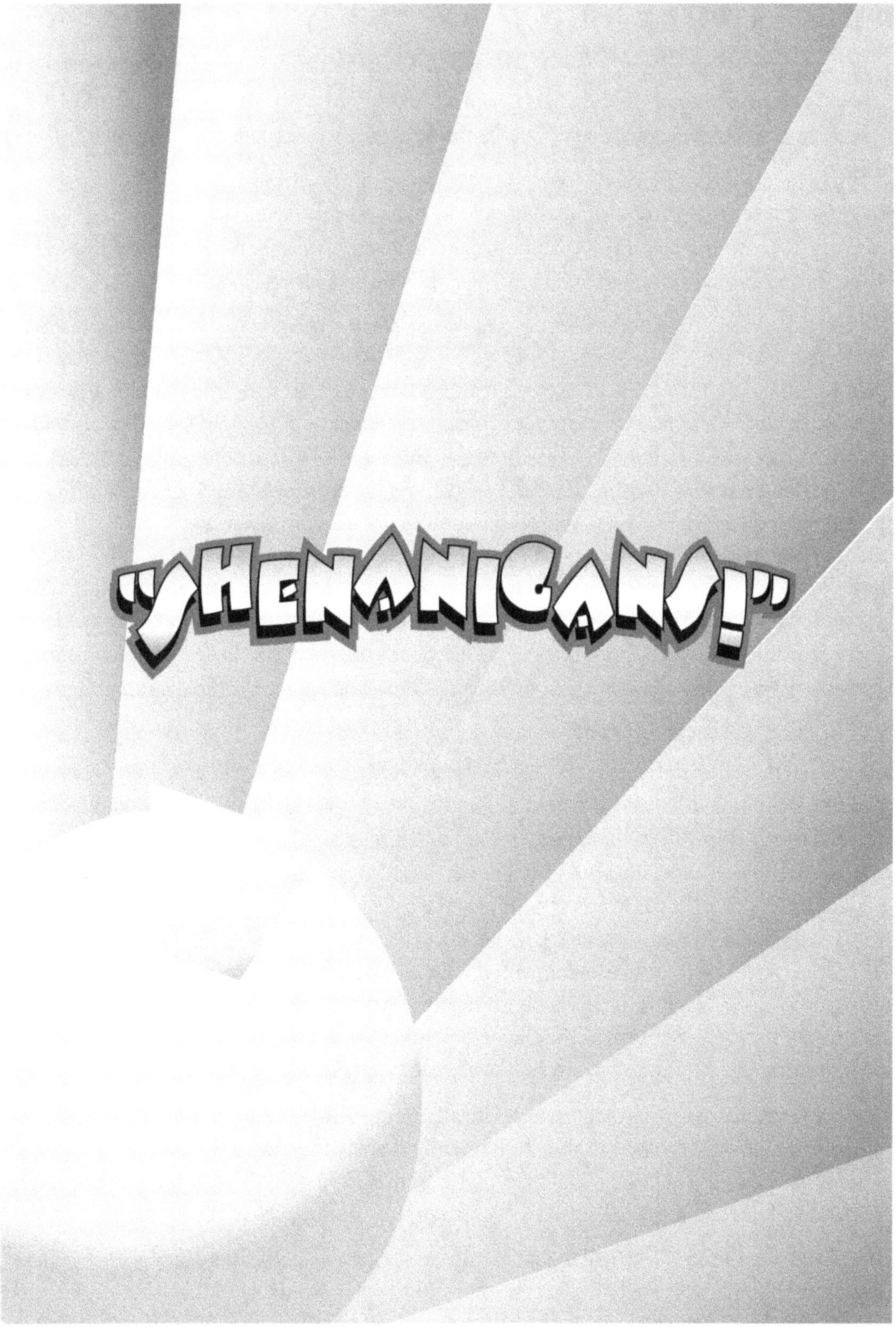
"SHENANIGANS!"

# Shenanigans! (2012)

*After a narrow escape from a band of Deer Creek river pirates, out-of-work wanderers Stuffy and Uncle Huggo think their fortune is made when they stumble across the pirates' treasure map...until it leads them to the Avery Elementary cafeteria. Posing as teachers, they quickly land jobs with the Adventure Club afterschool program thanks to a recent outbreak of armadillo flu that's put most of the staff on sick leave.*

*Their attempts to unearth the buried riches rouse the suspicions of Mr. Boondoggle, the afterschool leader, and his right-hand students, Chicarelli and Woobie, who wouldn't mind finding a little treasure for themselves if for no other reason than to buy some decent snacks instead of the unprocessed, organic ones served daily by Ms. Alfie, the Adventure Club administrator.*

*The search for the gold is on! And no matter which of these chuckleheads finds it, along the way there'll be plenty of Shenanigans!*

With my youngest in her last year at Avery, I realized it was a good chance this would be my last Avery Play. I wanted to do something big, something that would make the audiences each night laugh but also that might mean something to me. I was watching Bob Hope and Bing Crosby in *Road to Morocco* one evening and it hit me. I love old movies—why not an Avery Play written like one? I probably spent way too many Saturday afternoons as a kid and as an adult watching the Marx Brothers, Abbott & Costello, Hope & Crosby...way too many afternoons. But those comedies had such a wonderful style—the snappy dialogue, the screwball plots, the slapstick—and it's a kind of storytelling nobody does any more. So I decided it was something to introduce to the Avery kids of today, something that would bring nostalgic smiles to the parents and grandparents in the audience and fresh laughs to kids who've probably never seen this kind of comedy before. And so, with a little *Road to Morocco*, a bit of *A Night at the Opera*, a splash of *Duck Soup*, a slice of "Birthday Blues" and some *Naughty Nineties* and "Disorder in the Court" thrown in for fun, I wrote *Shenanigans!*

If you know those old movies, the characters of *Shenanigans!* will be familiar. If not, go watch the movies I listed—not only will they help you with the feel of the play, but they're also sidesplittingly funny. Though the characters in *Shenanigans!* can be played any way your actors choose, just for reference, Uncle Huggo and Stuffy are patterned on Bing Crosby and Bob Hope in their *Road* films, while Mr. Boondoggle, Chicarelli, Woobie, and Ms. Alfie could all easily be played by Groucho, Chico, and Harpo Marx and unofficial Marx brother Margaret Dumont (though Chicarelli also has a lot of Leo Gorcey's Slip Mahoney from the *Bowery Boys* to her). I didn't want to make Woobie a complete riff on Harpo Marx and make her mute, but I did want maintain that communication barrier that makes Harpo's interactions so much fun, so I came up with the idea that she only talks in complete non sequiturs. Keep in mind when casting that the sex of most of the characters can be easily swapped—in fact, my original script had a male Stuffy and a Mrs. Von Moldy; it was after casting we found the need to switch them and it went off perfectly.

This was the show where I wrote a small part specifically for myself. As "The Writer" I was able to wink at the audience myself through an ongoing gag that didn't so much break the fourth wall as twist it back around on itself. The performances were universally hilarious, Chicarelli's Mom and Mr. Von Moldy both showstoppers while Mr. Boondoggle, brought to life by my brother Brian, was a note-perfect turn in Groucho's shoes.

It was a great show to go out on. The final night was almost non-stop laughs, and you wouldn't believe how many grandparents from the audience caught me after the curtain to say how much fun it was to see that kind of story again. Here's my last Avery Play, a tribute to the zany comedies of the 1930s and 1940s that I've loved my whole life and wanted to share. Enjoy the shenanigans!

"SHENANIGANS!"


Written by

*Patrick Dorsey*

# "SHENANIGANS!"

CHARACTERS:

STUFFY, a ne'er-do-well on the lookout for opportunity.

UNCLE HUGGO, Stuffy's mentor and fellow wanderer.

MR. J. HUBERT BOONDOGGLE, killing time at Avery Adventure Club.

CHICARELLI, the head kid at Avery Adventure Club.

WOOBIE, the name says it all.

MS. ALFIE, as in charge of Avery Adventure Club as anyone can be.

RIVER PIRATES, Arr!

a CAPTIVE, in the wrong place at the wrong time.

The WRITER, every play needs at least one.

KIDS, because afterschool Adventure Club is crawlin' with 'em.

The ANNOUNCER, imparting commercial wisdom.

an AVERY STUDENT, who needs to work on numbers.

MR. VON MOLDY, the new -- and original -- Avery Principal.

CHICARELLI'S MOM, it's a Jersey thing.

PARENTS and GRANDPARENTS, because all the kids have 'em.

VAL, the totally tubular Adventure Club volunteer.

BETH, grand dame of the Avery stage.

AVERY PLAYERS, because we have some every year.

JUSTIN BIEBER, the young pop star everyone loves (right?)

THE CURLY CHORUS, nyuck, nyuck, nyuck!

DR. SMITH, enjoying the Avery Play.

THE MOST INTERESTING MAN IN WEBSTER GROVES, you know him.

a PIZZA GUY, just making a delivery and working for tips.

CAPTAIN BLACKPATCH, exploring alternate career options.

"SHENANIGANS"

ACT ONE


SCENE 1:

Some low BUSHES near DEER CREEK.

STUFFY and UNCLE HUGGO stumble into view, looking over their
shoulders.

> STUFFY
> Wow, Uncle Huggo, who'da ever thought we'd
> get ambushed by river pirates in Deer
> Creek?

> UNCLE HUGGO
> Stuffy, old kid, it's a strange, strange
> world! Nothing surprises me any more!

The RIVER PIRATES coast into view.

> PIRATE #1
> Arr!

> PIRATE #2
> Arr!

> PIRATE #3
> Avast!

> STUFFY
> You think they want us to play "One of
> These Things is Not Like the Others"?

> UNCLE HUGGO
> Hide!

They duck behind some bushes, peeking around to spy on the pirates.

> PIRATE #1
> (Squinting over the stage)
> The Cap'n 'll have our bandanas fer sure if
> we don't find those two!

> PIRATE #2
> And if he learns we lost the treasure map,
> too --

> PIRATE #1
> Ooh! Don't even talk about it! We haveta
> find a way to get those two back!

                    PIRATE #3
Let's try scarin' 'em!

                    PIRATE #1
How are we gonna do that? They escaped!

                    PIRATE #2
Make 'em worry for someone else!

                    PIRATE #1
Yeah -- we got that passenger we can hold
captive!

                    PIRATE #3
               (Dropping out of character)
But she booked this cruise through a travel
agent and everything!

                    PIRATE #1
So what? We're pirates! Arr!

                    PIRATE #2
Arr!

                    PIRATE #3
               (Back in character)
Aaaarrrr!

                    PIRATE #2
Go get 'er!

Pirate #3 runs off.

                    PIRATE #1
               (Calling out to the bushes)
Listen up, ya lily-livered lubbers!

                    STUFFY
Are they talking to us?

                    UNCLE HUGGO
To you -- like you always tell me, you're
not a fighter, you're a lubber.

                    STUFFY
Me and my irresistible good looks!

                    PIRATE #1
If you're not back here with our map by the
count of five --

Pirate #3 comes back with the CAPTIVE, her hands and knees tied
together.

                              PIRATE #1 (CONT'D)
                         (Calling out to the bushes)
          -- Then this one walks the plank!

                              CAPTIVE
          No! Oh, no!

The pirates laugh. One snorts and they all look at her, the mood
broken.

                              PIRATE #2
                         (Calling out to the bushes)
          Here we go!

Stuffy counts along on her fingers.

                              PIRATE #2 (CONT'D)
          One --
          Two --
          Five!

Stuffy does a double-take at her hand.

                              UNCLE HUGGO
          Math skills like that, no wonder they're
          only sailing Deer Creek!

                              STUFFY
                         (Waving her fingers)
          And here I was worried I'd sprouted two
          extra!

                              CAPTIVE
          Help! Help!

                              STUFFY
          What should we do, Uncle Huggo?

                              UNCLE HUGGO
          There's nothing we can do! It was all we
          could do to escape ourselves! We'll just
          end up captured again!

                              PIRATE #1
          All right, then -- She walks the plank!

                              CAPTIVE
          Oh no! Help!

She and the pirates disappear.

OS, the Captive lets out a loud, silly (like jumping in the pool)
scream, followed by the sound of a huge SPLASH!

                    UNCLE HUGGO
          Glad they're gone.

                    STUFFY
          Gee, Uncle Huggo, you think we did the
          right thing? She'll be all right, won't
          she?

                    UNCLE HUGGO
          Stuffy, she'll be fine. It's Deer Creek --
          the water's what, four inches deep?

The Captive shuffles across the stage, still tied up but barefoot,
her pants soaked to her calves.

                    CAPTIVE
          More like eight.

Stuffy and Uncle Huggo startle and grab each other as she continues
by, headed offstage.

                    CAPTIVE (CONT'D)
                (Sarcastic)
          Thanks for all your help!

She exits. Stuffy and Uncle Huggo shrug.

Stuffy reaches in her shirt and pulls out a large, old, ragged sheet
of paper and mops her forehead with it.

                    STUFFY
          That was a close one!

                    UNCLE HUGGO
          Say, what was all that talk of a map about?
          I never saw one!

                    STUFFY
          No idea!

Stuffy wipes her neck.

                    STUFFY (CONT'D)
          I mean, they are pirates -- don't they all
          get issued maps along with their
          telescopes, eyepatches, and hooks their
          first day on the job?

Stuffy starts to blow her nose when Uncle Hugo realizes what she's
about to blow it on and snatches the paper from her. Stuffy staggers
forward, all wind-up and no pitch.

                    STUFFY (CONT'D)
          Hey, a gal could wind up with whiplash from
          you doing that!

> UNCLE HUGGO
> Stuffy, you chowderhead, this is the map!

> STUFFY
> Really? I just grabbed it as we slipped
> out -- my allergies are killin' me!

Uncle Huggo disgustedly teases the map open.

> UNCLE HUGGO
> So I can see.
> (Looking it over)
> Look -- this shows the way to a treasure!

> STUFFY
> A treasure! Wing-ding! How do we find it?

> UNCLE HUGGO
> Let's see. It looks like we're here . . .

He points on the map, touching it, then without making a face, wipes his finger on Stuffy's shirt.

> STUFFY
> Hey, you know this thing's dry-clean only!

> UNCLE HUGGO
> I'd have thought you have to have it
> fumigated.

> STUFFY
> Only before special occasions.

Uncle Huggo turns the map over and around a few times

> UNCLE HUGGO
> This right here is the road we're standing
> on, and it looks like the treasure's right
> up the street, under some elementary school
> building --

> STUFFY
> A very elementary school. Says so on the map.

> UNCLE HUGGO
> That says "Avery Elementary School"!

> STUFFY
> Well, what are we standing around for?

> UNCLE HUGGO
> Fortune awaits!

> STUFFY
> We're off on the road to Avery!

> UNCLE HUGGO
> Off on another misadventure!

> STUFFY
> Up to our old shenanigans!

They start to walk off.

SOUND EFFECTS: MUSIC comes up.

They look like they're about break into song.

SOUND EFFECTS: A record scratch cuts off the music.

> WRITER (OS)
> Ahem!

Stuffy turns and winces as she sees THE WRITER enter, rubbing his thumb against his fingers like Stuffy owes him money.

> STUFFY
> Awwww --

Clearly disappointed, Stuffy pulls out a $5 bill as The Writer meets her center stage. Reluctant, stuffy hands the money over. The writer pockets it and walks off.

> UNCLE HUGGO
> What was that all about?

> STUFFY
> Oh, before the show I bet that guy five
> bucks that they wouldn't be able to work
> the title of the play into the first scene.

> UNCLE HUGGO
> Stuffy, you hodad, that's the writer!

> STUFFY
> Oh, wow! Don't I feel like a boob now!

> WRITER (OS)
> Ahem!

The Writer enters again, rubbing his fingers again.

Stuffy rolls her eyes and reluctantly pulls out another $5 and hands it to him. The Writer pockets the second bill and exits. Uncle Huggo just stares at Stuffy, waiting for an explanation.

> STUFFY
> I also bet him they couldn't get the word
> "boob" in before the end of the first scene
> either.

Uncle Huggo shakes his head as the two head off. Stuffy slips, but Uncle Huggo catches her before she falls.

UNCLE HUGGO
You okay?

STUFFY
Yeah, I just slipped on that old burrito in
the grass there.

They lean for a closer look, then Stuffy checks the bottom of her
shoe.

STUFFY (CONT'D)
At least I hope that was an old burrito.

Uncle Huggo sighs, and the two again head off, Stuffy dragging the
bottom of her one shoe on the ground as they walk away.

END SCENE 1.


SCENE 2:

The Avery Cafeteria, where they're currently having Adventure Club.
KIDS are sitting at tables doing homework, playing games.
MR. BOONDOGGLE sits at a table playing cards with two life-size
cardboard PHOTO CUT-OUTS of CHICARELLI and WOOBIE.

PA VOICE
And our final Avery announcement for today,
an update on the cafeteria hot lunch: It
was meat. (Beat) We'll have specific
results back from the lab in forty-eight
hours. Thanks, and have a great rest of the
day!

Mr. Boondoggle throws down his cards

MR. BOONDOGGLE
Gin! Now, pay up you ragamuffins!

MS. ALFIE, the Adventure Club administrator, enters with a big tray.
She places it on one of the tables.

MS. ALFIE
Children! It's snack time!

KIDS
(Excited)
Snack time! Snack time!

MS. ALFIE
We're having raw broccoli!

The kids all deflate. They shuffle over to the snack table.

>               KIDS
>          (Depressed)
>     Snack time . . . snack time . . .

>               MR. BOONDOGGLE
>          (To the cutouts)
>     C'mon you two hooligans, I've got gerbils
>     back home to feed!

>               MS. ALFIE
>     And there's cauliflower juice to drink!

Mr. Boondoggle watches the kids deflate still more.

While he's looking away, CHICARELLI and WOOBIE sneak in, grab their cut-outs, and start stashing them. Mr. Boondoggle turns and spots them.

>               MR. BOONDOGGLE
>     Well, that at least explains why you two
>     were playing so much better than usual.

The two kids startle, then finish stashing the cutouts.

>               MR. BOONDOGGLE (CONT'D)
>     Say, Chicarelli, those do seem pretty
>     handy -- where's a fella pick up one of
>     those, anyways?

>               CHICARELLI
>     Never you mind. Let's just say I know a guy.

>               MR. BOONDOGGLE
>     So what were you off doing? I mean, just so
>     I can be accurate when I have to testify at
>     sentencing after the trial.

>               CHICARELLI
>     I heard during recess that we weren't
>     getting actual snacks after school, and I
>     lined up a lead on some Jello.
>          (Points a thumb at the playground door)
>     They're waitin' outside for Woobie now.

Woobie gets up, looks around, and sneaks for the door.

>               MR. BOONDOGGLE
>     Woobie, grab me some Jello while you're out
>     there, too, would you?

Woobie happily gives an OK sign, two thumbs up, and a chest tap/peace sign and exits.

                    MR. BOONDOGGLE
So, Chicarelli, how long 'til your next
stint in detention?

                    CHICARELLI
What are you incinerating with that remark?

                    MR. BOONDOGGLE
Just looking out over the career path
you're headed down.

                    CHICARELLI
I've only been in trouble one time this
year.

                    MR. BOONDOGGLE
Good thing you have the whole rest of the
semester to catch up.

                    CHICARELLI
I had to go to the principal for being
propane in class.

                    MR. BOONDOGGLE
Propane?

                    CHICARELLI
Yeah -- using propanity and other bad words
in class.

Mr. Boondoggle is about to say something when Woobie slips back in
and, with bare hands, plops a handful of Jello in front of
Mr. Boondoggle and Chicarelli each.

                    MR. BOONDOGGLE
     Remind me to ask for a plate next time.

Woobie pulls a plate from inside the back of her pants, drops it in
front of Mr. Boondoggle, then picks up the Jello and slaps it down
on it.

                    MR. BOONDOGGLE (CONT'D)
     Thank you.

He pushes the plate aside.

                    MR. BOONDOGGLE (CONT'D)
     Remind me never to ask for utensils.

Chicarelli takes Mr. Boondoggle's Jello plate.

                    CHICARELLI
No sense letting it go to waste.

                    MR. BOONDOGGLE
          Now, hold the phone there. I don't think
          Woobie got any --

Woobie waves him off, reaching in a pocket and pulling out another
handful of Jello she starts eating like a runny apple.

                    MR. BOONDOGGLE (CONT'D)
          And here I was worried.
                    (To Chicarelli)
          Have at!

                    MS. ALFIE
          Oh, crackers and biscuits! Children, stop!
          We forgot -- everybody needs to get some
          hand sanitizer right now!

She takes a bottle and starts squirting some in each kid's hands.

                    MS. ALFIE (CONT'D)
          Remember: to make sure your hands are
          clean, rub them together for as long as it
          takes to sing "Happy Birthday."

                    MS. ALFIE AND KIDS
                    (All together)
          Happy birthday, happy birthday to you,
          happy birthday, happy birthday to you --

                    CHICARELLI
          Aw, do we have to?

                    MR. BOONDOGGLE
          Besides, it's not like kids are ever clean.

                    MS. ALFIE
          All the more reason -- We're at the height
          of flu season! Do you have any idea what
          awful things are going around?

                    MR. BOONDOGGLE
          You mean besides the ones the parents pick
          up here between now and six?

                    MS. ALFIE
          There's bird flu, swine flu -- I hear
          there's a terrible armadillo flu out there
          this year!

                    PA VOICE
          Ms. Alfie, please report to the Main
          Office, Ms. Alfie, to the Main Office.

                    MS. ALFIE
        Mr. Boondoggle, be a dear and take over
        while I run up to the office?

She hands him the bottle before he can respond.

                    MS. ALFIE (CONT'D)
        Now, I trust you have everything --

                    MR. BOONDOGGLE
        Never had any complaints.

                    MS. ALFIE
        I shouldn't be long.

She exits.

                    MR. BOONDOGGLE
        Armadillo flu. Hmph! Sounds like something
        they'd make up for an Avery play.

He squirts a few more kids' hands, and the children drift off to do
other things, leaving Chicarelli and Woobie with him. They look at
one another, shrug, and start to walk off without using the
sanitizer.

                    CHICARELLI
        Ah, she's just being melodrastic.

                    MR. BOONDOGGLE
        Poppycock, I say --

SOUND EFFECTS: Someone clearing their throat.

They all three hurry back to the table, squirt sanitizer into their
hands and start rubbing them together.

                    MR.BOONDOGGLE/CHICARELLI
                    (Together, quiet and quick)
        Happy birthday, happy birthday, to you,
        Happy birthday, happy birthday, to you,
        Happy birthday, happy birthday,
        Happy birthday to you!

                    WOOBIE
        Where's the beef?!?

They start to walk off again, pretending like they didn't do
anything.

                    CHICARELLI
        She's was just getting' historical.

                    MR. BOONDOGGLE
        Poppycock and balderdash, I tell you.

SOUND EFFECTS: A sneeze.

They all three rush back to the table, squirt more sanitizer and rub it hurried, panicky into their hands and up their arms.

> MR.BOONDOGGLE/CHICARELLI
> (Together, nervously pretending
> not to be scared)
> Happy birthday, happy birthday, to you,
> Happy birthday, happy birthday, to you,
> Happy birthday, happy birthday,
> Happy birthday to you!

> WOOBIE
> Your seats may also be used as a flotation
> device.

They start to walk off again like nothing happened, like they're congratulating themselves.

> CHICARELLI
> A pigment of the imagination.

> MR. BOONDOGGLE
> Poppycock, balderdash, hogwash, and maybe
> even tomfoolery! I'm not sure --

SOUND EFFECTS: A violent cough, all horky and phlegmy.

The three scramble back to the table, pawing over one another, freaked out and fighting over the sanitizer, pumping the bottle over their hands and arms, rubbing it into their faces -- Woobie even squirts it in her mouth.

> MR.BOONDOGGLE/CHICARELLI
> (Together, almost shouting
> and freaked out)
> Happy birthday, happy birthday, to you,
> Happy birthday, happy birthday,to you,
> Happy birthday, happy birthday,
> Happy birthday to you!

> WOOBIE
> I have a nickel for the parking meter!

They all stand and wait, listening for another awful, sick sound.

> MR. BOONDOGGLE
> If you hear anybody hurling, let me know so
> I can leave for the day.

> CHICARELLI
> Ah, that's bugwash!

MR. BOONDOGGLE

Bugwash?

CHICARELLI

Well, that's what you called it.

MR. BOONDOGGLE

I said "hogwash."

CHICARELLI

What's a hog?

MR. BOONDOGGLE

What do you mean, "What's a hog?"

CHICARELLI

What is it?

MR. BOONDOGGLE

Seriously? You don't know what a hog is?

Chicarelli shakes her head.

MR. BOONDOGGLE (CONT'D)

The state of our educational system . . .
          (To Woobie)
You know what a hog is, don't you?

Woobie leans over, and very innocently puts her head on
Mr. Boondoggle's chest and hugs him.

CHICARELLI

He said "hog" not "hug"!

Ms. Alfie returns, with papers in hand, leading in Stuffy and
Uncle Huggo.

MS. ALFIE

You simply have no idea how lucky it is you
two showed up when you did -- We just had
two of our Adventure Club leaders go on
extended sick leave.

Chicarelli and Woobie start for the hand sanitizer. Mr. Boondoggle
shakes his head and they stop.

MR. BOONDOGGLE

I think we milked that bit for all it
was worth.

STUFFY

Well like they say, timing's everything!
          (To Uncle Huggo)
Not to mention keeping a flash drive full
of fake resumes handy!

>                    UNCLE HUGGO
> Shh!

>                    MS. ALFIE
> And to have two such accomplished people
> drop out of the sky and into our proverbial
> lap like this!

She glances at the papers.

>                    MS. ALFIE (CONT'D)
> Degrees from Princeton and Rennselaar
> Polytechnic Institute -- and a Ph.D from
> Pepperdine University!

Stuffy and Uncle Huggo nod their heads, going along with her.

>                    MS. ALFIE (CONT'D)
> Members of Mensa, and -- the Kennedy
> family!!

>                    UNCLE HUGGO
> Distant cousins, really.

>                    STUFFY
> But not so distant that we didn't get to
> help with Uncle Teddy's empties at the
> holidays.

>                    MS. ALFIE
> Starting pitcher for the 1974 Washington
> Senators!

Stuffy does a double-take at Uncle Huggo.

>                    UNCLE HUGGO
>              (Out of the side of his mouth)
> Nobody remembers that team.

>                    MS. ALFIE
> And you had your own talk show on the Oprah
> Winfrey Network!

>                    STUFFY
>              (Modest)
> Oh, it's not like anybody watches that
> channel!

>                    MS. ALFIE
>              (Indicates Uncle Huggo)
> Roller coaster architect
>              (Indicates Stuffy)
>  -- and board-certified proctologist!

                    STUFFY
                (To Uncle Huggo)
        That is one of those baby-delivering
        doctors, right?

                    UNCLE HUGGO
        Not quite. Same neighborhood, though.

                    MS. ALFIE
        But this, this I can't believe -- Stuffy
        and Uncle Huggo look suddenly worried,
        caught.

                    MS. ALFIE (CONT'D)
        -- I can't believe it at all: decorated
        military heroes of the French Foreign
        Legion!

                    STUFFY
        Well, that's our story and we're stickin'
        to it!

Uncle Huggo nudges her. Ms. Alfie doesn't react to either.

                    MS. ALFIE
        I mean, what are the odds?

She moves between them. They look ready to bolt.

                    MS. ALFIE (CONT'D)
        My dear, dear papa was a legionnaire!

She hooks her arms onto each of theirs.

                    MS. ALFIE
        Come on, sing along --
        *Nous sommes des dégourdis,*
        *Nous sommes des lascars --*

She cheerfully makes them march in place with her as the two fake the
French and cheerfulness and pretend to sing along.

                    MS. ALFIE (CONT'D)
        *-- Des types pas ordinaires.*
        *Nous avons souvent notre cafard,*
        *Nous sommes des legionnaires!*

                    UNCLE HUGGO
        Good times, good times . . .

                    MS. ALFIE
        Now, we are a secure building, and we'll
        need to get you some IDs. In the
        meantime --

She hands peel-off sticky badges to Uncle Huggo, then Stuffy.

                    MS. ALFIE (CONT'D)
          -- you'll need these sticky badges.

                    STUFFY
          Badges? Badges? We don't need no sticky
          badges!

She pitches hers on the floor. Ms. Alfie and Uncle Huggo just stare
at her.

Stuffy, sorry, picks it back up and starts to put it on.

                    STUFFY
          It was funny in rehearsal.

                    PA VOICE
          Ms. Alfie, please come to the front of the
          school, Ms. Alfie to the pick-up/drop-off
          at the front of the school.

                    MR. BOONDOGGLE
                    (To Chicarelli)
          Maybe that's your ride.

                    CHICARELLI
          Nah, my mom can't drive right now -- doctor
          says she has carpool tunnel syndrome.

                    MS. ALFIE
          If you'll excuse me, I'll leave you to
          introduce yourselves to the children and
          our afterschool leaders.

She exits. Stuffy and Uncle Huggo look the room up and down, casing
it on the sly.

                    STUFFY
                    (To Uncle Huggo, quietly)
          So this is the place.

                    UNCLE HUGGO
          A fortune in pirate treasure buried
          somewhere in here. We just have to figure
          out how to find it.

                    STUFFY
          Well, in the meantime, we better make
          friendly with the local pygmies.

                    UNCLE HUGGO
                    (To the kids, over-friendly)
          Hi there! You kids can call me Uncle Huggo.

                    STUFFY
          And I'm Stuffy --

A KID just stands up, holds out his backpack, drops it, and walks off
in disgust.

                    STUFFY
          What'd I say?

                    UNCLE HUGGO
          You have that effect on people.

                    CHICARELLI
          Yeah, probably because of your <u>face</u>.

She starts to high-five Woobie.

                    STUFFY
          Ah, you must be the short, annoying kid I
          ordered.
                    (To Uncle Huggo)
          They must've forwarded the package!

                    UNCLE HUGGO
                    (To the others)
          Just wrap her back up in the box she came
          in and we'll throw it in my trunk. Oh, and
          make sure the air holes in that box are
          plugged tight!

Mr. Boondoggle gets up and approaches far too seriously.

                    MR. BOOONDOGGLE
          Sir, I like the cut of your jib, sir!

He shakes Uncle Huggo's hand solemnly.

                    MR. BOOONDOGGLE (CONT'D)
          J. Hubert Boondoggle, Senior, at your
          service.

                    UNCLE HUGGO
          Mr. Boondoggle --

                    MR. BOONDOGGLE
          The feeling's mutual.

Stuffy shakes his hand.

                    STUFFY
          Say, how old's your son?

                    MR. BOONDOGGLE
          What son?

                    STUFFY
          You said J. Hubert Boondoggle senior, which
          kinda implies there's a junior . . . ?

                    MR. BOONDOGGLE
          Oh, not yet. I'm just planning ahead. Stuck
          with a name like this my whole life, I'm
          gonna make darn certain somebody else has
          to put up with it, too!

                    CHICARELLI
          Yeah, just like everyone has to put up with
          your face!

                    MR. BOONDOGGLE
          Y'know, we don't need to wait for a box to
          start plugging air holes . . .

She flinches playfully, then offers her hand to Uncle Huggo.

                    CHICARELLI
          Chicarelli, fifth grade. I'm the head kid
          at Adventure Club. This here's Woobie.

Uncle Huggo starts to shake Woobie's hand.

                    WOOBIE
          Next time, I'm coloring in the lines.

She hugs Uncle Huggo the way she did Mr. Boondoggle.

                    UNCLE HUGGO
          I get it -- because I'm Uncle Hugg-o.

                    STUFFY
          Then I guess I better keep my distance.

Woobie hugs her, too. It goes on for a Beat, uncomfortably long, as
Stuffy tries unsuccessfully to wriggle away.

                    UNCLE HUGGO
          So, what do you kids do for fun around
          here?

                    STUFFY
          You ever play pirates and search for lost
          treasure?

Uncle Huggo swats at her. Woobie's still glued to Stuffy.

                    CHICARELLI
          Since Ms. Alfie came, we get presenters
          every couple days to show us stuff -- she
          says you can observe a lot by watching.

                  MR. BOONDOGGLE
Or something like that.

                  CHICARELLI
A magician's coming next week. He's going
to show us how to saw a lady in half --

Woobie's still stuck to Stuffy.

                  STUFFY
Yeah, but will he show you how to hide the
remains?

                  CHICARELLI
        (Doesn't get it)
-- and how to pull a rabbit out of your
pants!

Mr. Boondoggle starts to comment but Uncle Huggo shakes his head.

                  UNCLE HUGGO
        (Aside)
Sorry folks, we're not doing those kinds of
jokes this year.

                  STUFFY
Funny kinda person to learn stuff from.

She finally wriggles free of Woobie.

                  CHICARELLI
That's what I told Ms. Alfie.

                  MR. BOONDOGGLE
Oh, come now -- You can learn all sorts of
things from anyone!

                  CHICARELLI
Anyone?

                  MR. BOONDOGGLE
Sure. Like Lydia. I learned so much from
her . . .

                  CHICARELLI
Who's Lydia?

                  MR. BOONDOGGLE
You mean you don't know Lydia?

Everyone around shrugs.

                  MR. BOONDOGGLE (CONT'D)
Then let me tell you all about her!

MUSICAL NUMBER:

A dance performance to "Lydia the Tattooed Lady"


END SCENE 2.


COMMERCIAL #1

                ANNOUNCER
     "Shenanigans!" will continue, right after
     this.

An AVERY STUDENT stumbles out on stage, looking shoved or tripped.

                ANNOUNCER
     Hey, kid, what's the highest number you can
     think of?

                AVERY STUDENT
     Sixty-one.

                ANNOUNCER
     No.

                AVERY STUDENT
     Five hundred ninety seven!

                ANNOUNCER
     No, I think you can go higher.

                AVERY STUDENT
     Three hundred? (Beat) Six hundred seventy-
     three?

                ANNOUNCER
     Higher still!

                AVERY STUDENT
     Nine million!

                ANNOUNCER
     Nope!

                AVERY STUDENT
     Nine million and, uh --five!

                ANNOUNCER
     Nuh-uh.

                AVERY STUDENT
     Oh I'm stumped!

                    ANNOUNCER
          And that's why you need the new
          Encyclopedia of Numbers -- a complete guide
          to every number in the world.

A GIANT BOOK is handed through the curtain to the kid.

                    ANNOUNCER (CONT'D)
          Come on, pick any number.

                    AVERY STUDENT
                  (Flipping through the book, amazed)
          Eleven thousand, one hundred eleven . . . A
          billion and ninety six . . . Four?!? Wow!

                    ANNOUNCER
          See? They're all right there! And new
          volumes are released quarterly as science's
          knowledge of numbers continues to expand.
          The Avery Student keeps flipping through
          it, astonished.

                    ANNOUNCER (CONT'D)
          Professionally arranged numerically for
          easy reference, the Encyclopedia of Numbers
          can be yours for only ten easy payments of
          $69.35, plus shipping and handling, and the
          quarterly update volumes each for two easy
          payments of $29.95.

                    AVERY STUDENT
          I'm gonna go home right now and pester my
          parents until they get me one!

The Avery Student dashes off.

                    ANNOUNCER
          The Encyclopedia of Numbers, from Kirkwood
          Publishing. Order yours today!

                                        END COMMERCIAL.


SCENE 3:

Adventure Club in the Avery Cafeteria. Chicarelli and the kids are
taking things in and out of the ADVENTURE CLUB TOY BOX, a big box set
on a table. Stuffy stares intently at a THING next to the box.
Uncle Huggo enters as Chicarelli crosses the room and trips over
something behind one of the other props.

                    CHICARELLI
          Stupid witch!

               UNCLE HUGGO
Excuse me, young lady?

               CHICARELLI
         (Confused)
What?

From behind the prop, she picks up an oversized WITCH HALLOWEEN DECORATION.

               CHICARELLI (CONT'D)
    Somebody left this stupid thing layin' out!

She returns it to the box and Uncle Huggo follows.

               UNCLE HUGGO
         (To Stuffy)
What you got there, Stuffy?

               STUFFY
    I don't know.

The Thing moves on its own.

SOUND EFFECTS: Stymie Surprise Cake noise ("Wheep-wow").

They all startle and back off, except Stuffy, who's spellbound and unmoving.

The Thing moves again.

SOUND EFFECTS: Stymie Surprise Cake noise -- twice.

Everyone but Stuffy starts to back away slowly.

Stuffy picks up the Thing.

               UNCLE HUGGO
    Good thinking, Stuffy, why don't you run
    that outside?

               STUFFY
    I wasn't going to --

SOUND EFFECTS: Stymie Surprise Cake noise.

               MR. BOONDOGGLE
    I think it wants to go.

SOUND EFFECTS: Stymie Surprise Cake noise.

               UNCLE HUGGO
    Yeah, right now!

               STUFFY
    Okay.

Stuffy leaves with it.

SOUND EFFECTS: Stymie Surprise Cake noise.

Relieved, everyone moves closer. Chicarelli and Woobie root through the box. Woobie pulls out a large SEA SHELL.

> CHICARELLI
> Cool! A sea shell. It sounds like the ocean if you hold it to yourear *(note: be sure to run the words together)*.

Woobie shrugs and puts the seashell on her behind and waits, listening intently.

> CHICARELLI (CONT'D)
> No! Your. Ear.

Woobie nods and pulls the shell off her behind.

SOUND EFFECTS: Pop!

Confused, Woobie looks it over and then returns it to the box. Chicarelli pulls a BOOMERANG from the box.

> CHICARELLI (CONT'D)
> Hey, look -- a stick.

Woobie goes back to rooting through the box.

> CHICARELLI (CONT'D)
> Who'd put that in the box?

> WOOBIE
> Spread the peanut butter all the way to the crust.

> CHICARELLI
> Ms. Alfie wouldn't want the Kindergarten kids playing with this. Throw it outside, wouldja?

She hands Woobie the boomerang and goes back to looking through the box.

Woobie throws the boomerang offstage, into one of the wings.

From the opposite wing, the boomerang flies in, dropping near Chicarelli. She turns and sees it on the floor.

> CHICARELL
> Hey! Didn't I ask you to throw that out?

> WOOBIE
> Pure Alpaca wool.

Woobie throws it back the way it came, and the boomerang flies in from the opposite side and lands behind Chicarelli.

>           CHICARELLI
>       Hey! I asked you to get rid of that. Stop
>       procrasterbating and throw it out!

>           WOOBIE
>       Cows go "Moo!"

Woobie throws it back the way it came, and the boomerang flies in
from the opposite side and lands behind Chicarelli.

Chicarelli spots it on the floor.

>           CHICARELLI
>       Forget it, Woobie. I'll do it myself!

Chicarelli throws it in the wings --

>           CHICARELLI (CONT'D)
>       I mean, what if one of the little kids
>       found that? Someone could get hurt!

-- And the boomerang comes back from the opposite side and smacks her
hard, square in the back!

>           CHICARELLI
>       Oww!

>           WOOBIE
>       Four out of five dentists surveyed
>       recommend sugarless gum for their patients
>       who chew gum.

>           CHICARELLI
>          (Rubbing her back)
>       I'll just put this in the trash.

She carefully walks the boomerang to the trash can and sets it in
there, backing away like she's training a puppy to stay.

Ms. Alfie enters. Chicarelli exits while Uncle Huggo watches
Ms. Alfie and Mr. Boondoggle.

>           MS. ALFIE
>       Oh, Mr. Boondoggle --

Mr. Boondoggle lights up.

>           MR. BOONDOGGLE
>       Oh, you can call me "J. Hubert."

>           MS. ALFIE
>       Mr. Boondoggle, I have a meeting to get to.
>          (Whispers)
>       Some very important budget talks concerning
>       the funding for Adventure Club --

                    MR. BOONDOGGLE
          Funding! Budgets!

                     MS. ALFIE
          Shh! It's nothing yet, so no need for any
          worries. In the meantime, Homework Club's
          about to start and the children need a
          tutor -- Be a peach and take charge of it
          for me while I'm gone, would you?

                    MR. BOONDOGGLE
          Why, of course. And maybe later, we
          might --

                     MS. ALFIE
          Woobie, dear, help me with my coat, would
          you?

Woobie runs to the closet and returns with an OVERSIZED OVERCOAT.
She starts to help Ms. Alfie on with it. Ms. Alfie gets one arm in
and keeps circling after Woobie to get the other in.

                  MS. ALFIE (CONT'D)
          No, circle this way, Woobie!

Woobie circles back and inside the coat, and they end up both
wearing the coat, side by side, each with an arm in a sleeve.

                  MS. ALFIE (CONT'D)
          This way, Woobie, and around --

Woobie ducks under Ms. Alfie so she ends up with one sleeve on
and the other wrapped under her and between her legs.

                  MS. ALFIE (CONT'D)
          Up here!

They circle some more, Ms. Alfie swapping sleeves and getting the
second one on so she ends up in the coat but with it backwards.

                  MS. ALFIE (CONT'D)
          No, this is backwards!

Woobie tugs a sleeve off her. They both turn, and Ms. Alfie ends
up with one sleeve on and the whole coat wrapped around her neck
and head.

                  MS. ALFIE (CONT'D)
                    (Muffled)
          Mff! Mmmff! Mff!

Woobie pulls the whole coat off her, getting it turned inside out
before helping her on with it.

> MS. ALFIE (CONT'D)
> Finally!
>> (Notices it's inside-out)
> Oh, bananas and cheddar, Woobie!

> WOOBIE
> My mom likes gladiator movies.

Woobie pulls the coat off her, puts it right-side out, and gets one sleeve on Ms. Alfie.

> MS. ALFIE
> Please, Woobie, I'm in a hurry!

Woobie wraps herself under the coat, getting the other sleeve on Ms. Alfie but ending up behind her inside the coat.

> MS. ALFIE (CONT'D)
> Well, I can't wait any longer!

She marches off, Woobie under the coat, pressed to her back, and exits.

Woobie runs back in

> WOOBIE
> Ham. Squirrel. Woof!

Uncle Huggo sidles next to Mr. Boondoggle as some Kids crawl in on their hands and knees, studying the floor.

> UNCLE HUGGO
> Say, you're sweet on her, aren't you?

> MR. BOONDOGGLE
> All right, you dragged it out of me. Yes, yes I am! She's the most wonderful person I ever met, and I look forward to settling down with her one day and having two-point-five kids together -- two for her and me to raise, and point five to creep out the nosy neighbors so they'll stay away.

> UNCLE HUGGO
> Yeah, she doesn't seem to get that. She ever shown the slightest interest back?

> MR. BOONDOGGLE
> Well, there was that once at snack time, when she accidentally dumped butterscotch pudding and tater tots all down the front of me.

> UNCLE HUGGO
> Perfect. And when you feel ready to move
> this up to "creepy" I've got a pair of
> binoculars you can borrow.

Stuffy enters in a pirate hat, eyepatch, and hook hand, along with Chicarelli, also in a pirate hat.

> CHICARELLI
> Arrr! Move it, ya scurvies, or it's
> keelhaulin' for the lot of ya!

> UNCLE HUGGO
> Hey there, Stuffy, what's, ah, --

> STUFFY
> She's a natural, isn't she?

> MR. BOONDOGGLE
> What are you fellas up to over here?

> STUFFY
> Well, we're not looking for lost pirate
> treasure.

Behind Mr. Boondoggle, Uncle Huggo starts shaking his head and giving a hand-across-the-throat "quit talking" signal.

> MR. BOONDOGGLE
> (Looking him up and down)
> Now, how could I ever come to such an
> insane conclusion? You should take a good
> look at yourself in the mirror.

> STUFFY
> Why would I want to hurt my feelings like
> that?
> (To Uncle Huggo)
> And why are you giving me our secret "stop
> talking" signal?

Uncle Huggo throws his hands in the air.

> MR. BOONDOGGLE
> It seems a very interesting game.

> STUFFY
> Oh, the kids love it.

> MR.BOONDOGGLE
> (Suspicious)
> Think I could play?

>                    STUFFY
>          Well, I'm not sure --
>
>                    UNCLE HUGGO
>          It's really for the kids --
>
>                    STUFFY
>          And it looks like we've got all the swabs
>          this deck can fit, what with all the
>          barnacles and grog --
>
>                    CHICARELLI
>          Everybody -- look busy! Mr. Von Moldy's on
>          his way.
>
>                    STUFFY
>          Who?
>
>                    MR. BOONDOGGLE
>          The interim principal.

He grabs a book and heads to the WHITEBOARD, donning a tasseled mortarboard.

>                    MR. BOONDOGGLE (CONT'D)
>          Gotta look busy when he's around -- he's
>          old-fashioned --
>
>                    CHICARALLI
>          He's just old. Came out of retirement to
>          help out. He was Avery's first principal!
>
>                    UNCLE HUGGO
>          First principal? But the school's like a
>          hundred years old --
>
>                    MR. BOONDOGGLE
>          It's been Avery since 1916, but who's
>          counting.

Stuffy's counting on her fingers.

>                    UNCLE HUGGO
>          -- that'd make him --
>
>                    STUFFY
>          -- two years older than dirt! Hold on,
>          Uncle Huggo -- this might turn in to
>          another "Thriller" send-up!

Mr. Boondoggle shushes them. As everyone takes their places,

MR. VON MOLDY shuffles in, ridiculously, painfully slow.

> MR. VON MOLDY
>
> Oh, don't mind me. I just like to come down
> at the end of the day and check on . . .

They all wait for her to finish. She keeps shuffling quietly forward.
After a Beat --

> MR. BOONDOGGLE
>
> Mr. Von Moldy?

> MR. VON MOLDY
>
> Hmm? Oh, don't mind me. I just like to come
> down at the end of the day and check
> on . . .

They all wait for her to finish. He keeps shuffling quietly forward.
After a Beat --

> MR. BOONDOGGLE
>
> Ah, Mr. Von Moldy -- stopping by to check
> up on us?

> MR. VON MOLDY
>
> Oh, yes. I just like to come down at the
> end of the day!

> MR. BOONDOGGLE
>
> You're just in time -- we're about to start
> Homework Club. Please, have a seat.

Mr. Von Moldy toddles to a nearby chair. Head down, he starts to
lower himself into the seat, but stops, midway, stuck.

> MR. VON MOLDY
>
> Give me a push, would you dear?

Uncle Huggo leans over, puts his hand on Mr. Von Moldy's forehead,
and nudges him. He rocks stiffly back into the chair.

> MR. BOONDOGGLE
>
> All right, now who's got homework they want
> to review?

> KID
>
> I have some math from Ms. French.

> MR. BOONDOGGLE
>
> Ah, Ms. French. I go to her room and listen
> to her lesson every afternoon I need a nap.

> KID
>
> I have a question.

> MR. BOONDOGGLE
>
> What is it?

> KID
> It's an interrogative statement used to
> test knowledge, but that's not important
> right now.

> UNCLE HUGGO
> Oh, these kids are quick!

Stuffy's taking notes. Chicarelli nods off.

> MR. BOONDOGGLE
> Hey, I'm the one who's supposed to be
> cutting up around here. Questions are
> important. They helps us learn, help us
> think -- help us learn to think! Like,
> "What color eyes will Felicity have if
> mother's wearing chiffon and father's
> wearing seersucker?" Charmeuse? Or "How
> long do you have to wait in line?"

Woobie's hand shoots up to answer. Mr. Boondoggle doesn't see.

> MR. BOONDOGGLE (CONT'D)
> "How long is a piece of string?

Woobie's hand shoots up to answer. Mr. Boondoggle doesn't see.

> MR. BOONDOGGLE (CONT'D)
> "How high can the sycamore grow?"

Woobie's hand shoots up to answer. Mr. Boondoggle doesn't see.

> MR. BOONDOGGLE (CONT'D)
> (Singing "Colors of the Wind" -- poorly)
> "If you cut it down you will neeeeeeever
> knooow . . . " Can't quite hit that note.
> Speaking of notes, how about the ones I
> took in Ms. French's math class.

He goes to the white board and draws a circle.

> MR. BOONDOGGLE (CONT'D)
> Now, this is zero. In Uncle Huggo's school
> days, they called it "naught" and it was
> made from cast iron.
> (Drawing equations on the board)
> If naught multiplied by naught is naught,
> what kind of knot should you use to tie
> your shoes?

Woobie's hand shoots up to answer. Mr. Boondoggle doesn't see.

                    MR. BOONDOGGLE (CONT'D)
          And if dividing by naught is unsolvable,
          then explain to me how my tie ended up like
          this. The answer?

Woobie jumps up.

                    MR. BOONDOGGLE AND WOOBIE
                         (Together)
          Asparagus!

                    UNCLE HUGGO
          I hope you're getting all this down.

                    STUFFY
          Just so later I can enjoy burning it.

                    MR. BOONDOGGLE
          Well, I think that's all you can handle for
          the day. I know I can't stomach any more.
          Oh Mr. Von Moldy, I believe you're wanted
          in the office.

                    MR. VON MOLDY
          The office? What is it?

                    MR. BOONDOGGLE
          It's that set of rooms upstairs where they
          make all the --
                         (Air quotes)
          -- "vital decisions" for the school. But
          that's not important right now.

                    KID
          Hey!

Chicarelli snores, then startles awake.

                    CHICARELLI
                         (Frantic)
          Is the play over?

Woobie pats her arm, reassuring.

                    WOOBIE
          I can't sit right after I eat Mexican food.

                    MR. BOONDOGGLE
          Here, Mr. Von Moldy, let's help you up.

He waves Woobie and Chicarelli over to help him with him. After a bit
of rocking and moving the chair, they get him to his feet.

He turns and pats at the chair, like he's feeling for something he
dropped.

>                    MR. VON MOLDY
>          At my age, you have to make sure everything
>          gets up with you!

>                    MR. BOONDOGGLE
>          Ah, it was nice of you to stop by and
>          visit!

He starts toddling off, even slower than before.

>                    MR. BOONDOGGLE (CONT'D)
>          Good bye now! (Beat) Say hello to the
>          descendants when you get home!

He keeps shuffling.

>                    MR. BOONDOGGLE (CONT'D)
>          At this rate, I'll be his age by the time
>          he's out of here!

He claps his hands, and waves in from all directions a group of shuffling REALLY OLD GRANDPARENTS with walkers.

MUSICAL NUMBER:

A dance performance to "Every Day I'm Shufflin"

PARENTS come in and take their kids and the old folks, all of them waving to Uncle Huggo and Stuffy who wave back until it's just the two of them and Chicarelli.

>                    UNCLE HUGGO
>               (To Chicarelli)
>          Stuck here for another overnight, huh?

>                    CHICARELLI
>          Ha, ha -- and so's your face!

CHICARELLI'S MOM enters, a real "Jersey Shore" type in big sunglasses, too-high heels, and leopard prints.

>                    CHICARELLI'S MOM
>          Pookie-bear, I got you all signed out up
>          front. It's time to go home!

>                    CHICARELLI
>          Oh, mom -- we're playin' pirates an' I'm
>          the discipline officer!

                    CHICARELLI'S MOM
        And I'm sure that's lots of fun, but we
        need to hurry -- our new reality show
        starts filming tonight.

                    UNCLE HUGGO
        Did she say "reality" or "surreality?"

                    STUFFY
        Let's find out what night it's on so we can
        unplug the TV.

                    CHICARELLI'S MOM
        Oh, what's this all over your face?

She produces a tissue, licks it a few times, and proceeds to wipe
Chicarelli's face with it.

                    CHICARELLI
        Is that spit?

                    CHICARELLI'S MOM
                (Duh)
        Yeah.

Chicarelli huffs, resigned to the humiliation as her mom finishes
wiping her cheek.

                    CHICARELLI'S MOM (CONT'D)
        C'mon, we've got to get home and get Rolex
        and Timex fed before the camera crew gets
        there.

                    STUFFY
        Rolex and Timex?

                    CHICARELLI'S MOM
        Our dogs.

                    UNCLE HUGGO
        Those are funny names for dogs.

                    CHICARELLI'S MOM
        Not really. They're watch dogs.
                (To Chicarelli)
        Say g'bye hon, we gotta go!

                    CHICARELLI
        Bye!

Stuffy and Uncle Huggo wave as the two exit, leaving them alone.
Uncle Huggo starts searching around.

                    UNCLE HUGGO
Quick, while we've got the place to
ourselves. We've got to find that treasure!

                    STUFFY
I have a plan.

                    UNCLE HUGGO
I told you before, Justin Timberlake's not
calling you back.

                    STUFFY
I'm not talking about that.

                    UNCLE HUGGO
Oh, then --

                    STUFFY
Besides, that plan's changed.

                    UNCLE HUGGO
Yeah, that was a little  unrealistic for
you --

                    STUFFY
It's Tom Arnold now.

                    UNCLE HUGGO
Mu-u-u-ch better.

                    STUFFY
Yeah, well, speaking of much better, paste
your peepers on how this game of Treasure
Island paid out for ol' Long John Stuffy
here.

She digs in her pocket and produces a handful of GOLD COINS.

                    UNCLE HUGGO
Hey-seuss marimba! Stuffy, you found it!

                    STUFFY
Not all of it. But I've got a pretty good
idea where the rest has to be.

                    UNCLE HUGGO
Show me!

                    STUFFY
With any luck, there's plenty more where
that came from!

                    UNCLE HUGGO
Now that we know where to look.

Stuffy nods knowingly.

                    UNCLE HUGGO (CONT'D)
          Well, what are we waiting around here for?

Stuffy leads him away and they exit.

From the opposite side of the stage, Mr. Boondoggle peeks around and then enters.

                    MR. BOONDOGGLE
               (Aside)
          Very interesting!


                                        END SCENE 3.

                                        END ACT ONE.

ACT TWO

SCENE 1:

In front of the curtain. Uncle Huggo and Stuffy wander out.

                    UNCLE HUGGO
          Hey, Stuffy, I just got some concert
          tickets. A big show with three top bands
          from back in the day.

                    STUFFY
          I love rock concerts. What groups are
          playing?

                    UNCLE HUGGO
          I doubt you ever heard of them. They're
          from when I was in school. And musical
          groups had some funny names back then.

                    STUFFY
          Oh, rock bands have funny names now.
          Radiohead, Big Time Rush, Vampires
          Everywhere --

                    UNCLE HUGGO
          True.

                    STUFFY
          So what groups are playing?

                    UNCLE HUGGO
          Well, let's see, The Who's playing first,
          The Band second, and on third, Yes.

                    STUFFY
          I'm just askin' you about the concert.

                    UNCLE HUGGO
          I said The Who's playing first, The Band
          second, and on third, Yes.

                    STUFFY
          Do you know about the concert?

                    UNCLE HUGGO
          Of course I do.

                    STUFFY
          And you're not having one of your senior
          moments right now?

UNCLE HUGGO

Oh no.

STUFFY

But you don't know what groups are playing?

UNCLE HUGGO

Sure I do. It's printed on the tickets.

STUFFY

Well then, who's playing first?

UNCLE HUGGO

Yes.

STUFFY

I mean the group's name.

UNCLE HUGGO

The Who.

STUFFY

The group playing first.

UNCLE HUGGO

The Who.

STUFFY

I'm asking you who's playing first.

UNCLE HUGGO

That's the group's name.

STUFFY

That's who's name?

UNCLE HUGGO

Yes.

STUFFY

Okay . . . let's move along in the show.
What's the second group?

UNCLE HUGGO

The Band.

STUFFY

That's what I'm asking. What's the name of
the band --

UNCLE HUGGO

The Band.

STUFFY

-- that's playing second?

> UNCLE HUGGO
> The Band.

> STUFFY
> Okay, okay, let's try it this way: When they pay the group that's playing second, the band gets the money --

> UNCLE HUGGO
> Why shouldn't they? They always put on a great show.

Stuffy sputters

> STUFFY
> In the ads for the concert, how do they list the second group?

> UNCLE HUGGO
> The Band.

> STUFFY
> -- the one playing second --

> UNCLE HUGGO
> The Band.

> STUFFY
> The band?

> UNCLE HUGGO
> Yes.

Stuffy shakes her head, confused.

> STUFFY
> All I'm trying to find out is the band on first.

> UNCLE HUGGO
> No. The Band's on second.

> STUFFY
> I'm not asking you who's on second.

> UNCLE HUGGO
> The Who's on first.

Stuffy shakes her head, takes a big breath.

> STUFFY
> Okay, the band playing first -- ?

> UNCLE HUGGO
> No. The Band plays second.

                    STUFFY
I'm not asking you who plays second.

                    UNCLE HUGGO
The Who plays first.

                    STUFFY
             (Confused)
Yes?

                    UNCLE HUGGO
They're playing third. We're not talking
about them.

                    STUFFY
How did we get to the third act?

                    UNCLE HUGGO
You mentioned the band's name.

                    STUFFY
I did? Who plays third?

                    UNCLE HUGGO
No. The Who plays first.

                    STUFFY
The band on first?

                    UNCLE HUGGO
The Band's on second.

                    STUFFY
The band.

                    UNCLE HUGGO
Correct.

                    STUFFY
Yes!

                    UNCLE HUGGO
They play third.

                    STUFFY
Stay there!

                    UNCLE HUGGO
All right.

                    STUFFY
Now who plays third?

                    UNCLE HUGGO
Why do you insist on putting The Who on
third?

                    STUFFY
The band on third?

                    UNCLE HUGGO
No. The Band plays second.

                    STUFFY
Who plays second?

                    UNCLE HUGGO
The Who plays first.

                    STUFFY
Yes?

              STUFFY & UNCLE HUGGO
               (Together)
They play third . . .

                    STUFFY
Y'know, I'm in a band. I play drums. So
let's say we get to play in that concert.

                    UNCLE HUGGO
Oh, Stuffy, this is a big show -- that's
crazy talk!

                    STUFFY
               (Aside)
That he calls crazy talk.
               (To Uncle Huggo)
So, imagine they squeeze us into the
concert between who and the band playing
second?

                    UNCLE HUGGO
Now that's the first thing you've said
right.

                    STUFFY
I don't even know what I'm talking about!

Stuffy grits her teeth.

                    STUFFY
So we play after yes.

                    UNCLE HUGGO
No you don't, you play after the Who.

                    STUFFY
Yes.

                    UNCLE HUGGO
That's different.

                    STUFFY
          That's what I said! We play after who. Then
          the band plays after us, and then yes plays
          third.

Uncle Huggo nods along.

                    STUFFY (CONT'D)
          The audience leaps from their seats and
          gives a thunderous standing ovation! For
          what? I don't know!

                    UNCLE HUGGO
          Oh, Stuffy, calm down. Y'know, the worst
          concert experience I ever had was with Tom
          Jones.

                    STUFFY
          Tom Jones? "What's New Pussycat?" and
          "Delilah" Tom Jones?

                    UNCLE HUGGO
          Yep. He never performed.

                    STUFFY
          Not at all?

                    UNCLE HUGGO
          Didn't even show up.

                    STUFFY
          But he's such a pro -- That doesn't sound
          like him.

                    UNCLE HUGGO
          I didn't think so either. But one day, I
          ran into him --

                    STUFFY
          No!

                    UNCLE HUGGO
          -- at the airport. And I asked him about
          it.

                    STUFFY
          So, what'd he tell you?

                    UNCLE HUGGO
          He said, "It's not unusual."

Silence. Crickets chirping.

                    STUFFY
That was a long way to go for that joke.

                  UNCLE HUGGO
Remind me to take that up with your pal the
writer when he comes to collect on your
next bet.

                                        END SCENE 1.


SCENE 2:

Adventure Club. Kids and teachers are doing their things. VAL, her
arm in a SLING, works on a jigsaw puzzle on the table, clearly
flummoxed.

                   PA VOICE
And our final announcement: the school
board would like to remind you again to do
your best to score well on the next week's
state aptitude test or they'll all be sent
to jail. Thanks, and have a great rest of
the day!

Uncle Huggo approaches Chicarelli.

                  UNCLE HUGGO
So, whatcha got going on there, Chicarelli?

                  CHICARELLI
I can't decide if I'm in a problem-solving
mood or a problem-causing mood.

                  UNCLE HUGGO
Well, when you figure it out, let me know
so I can contact the appropriate
authorities.

                  CHICARELLI
And what's with snacks today? Sprouts and
wheatgrass?

                  UNCLE HUGGO
Gives a person the impression Ms. Alfie's
just bringing in whatever's stuck under her
lawnmower, doesn't it?

A Kid goes past, drinking from a cup with a lid and straw.

                  CHICARELLI
Hey, kid -- whatcha got there?

                              KID
            Smoothie.

                         CHICARELLI
            Where'd you get that? Never mind, lemme
            have some.

Before the Kid can object, Chicarelli takes it and puts the straw in
her mouth.

                    CHICARELLI (CONT'D)
            What flavor is it?

                              KID
                    (As Chicarelli sips it)
            Pickle.

Chicarelli does a spit take.

                         CHICARELLI
            Now I need some cow juice to get the taste
            out of my mouth.

                        UNCLE HUGGO
            You mean milk?

                         CHICARELLI
            What?

                        UNCLE HUGGO
            What comes from the cow's udder --

                         CHICARELLI
            Its other what?

                        UNCLE HUGGO
            I'm beginning to see why Boondoggle is the
            way he is.

                         CHICARELLI
            We went to a farm once and I got chased by
            this boy cow --

                        UNCLE HUGGO
            Bull --

                         CHICARELLI
            No, it really happened!

Chicarelli's Mom enters.

                      CHICARELLI'S MOM
            Hello everybody! I'm here to help out!

                    MS. ALFIE
Thank you so much! I think our high school
volunteer Val over there needs some
assistance.

                    CHICARELLI'S MOM
Okey-doke.

                    CHICARELLI
And then the farmer showed us his bees and
where they make their bee milk.

                    UNCLE HUGGO
Honey.

                    CHICARELLI'S MOM
Yes, sweetheart?

                    UNCLE HUGGO
I'm going to go find something less
stressful to do. Like letting Stuffy jab
needles in me again.

                    STUFFY
Hey! I got a C-minus and a certificate in
that acupuncture class!

                    UNCLE HUGGO
That teacher must've had a diploma quota
to fill.

                    CHICARELLI'S MOM
          (To Val)
Sorry I'm late -- I locked my keys in the
car and had to find a coat hanger to get it
unlocked.

                    VAL
Bogus, Mrs. C.!

                    CHICARELLI'S MOM
I know, right? The worst part was, I had to
hurry because it was starting to rain and
the top was down!
          (Notices the sling)
What happened to your arm, sweetie?

                    VAL
I got hurt raking leaves over the weekend.

                    CHICARELLI'S MOM
Oh no! What happened?

                    VAL
Well, I was raking leaves --

               CHICARELLI'S MOM
Yeah . . .

                    VAL
And my dad came out and goes "you're doing
it wrong," and I was like "no way" and he
was like "way" and I was like "no way" and
he was like "way" -- and then I fell out of
the tree!

               CHICARELLI'S MOM
Oh. My. Gawsh!

Woobie ambles over and hugs Chicarelli's Mom.

               CHICARELLI'S MOM
Oh! And how are you, Woobie-pumpkin?

                  WOOBIE
Dadaism is an anarchist rejection of
prevailing cultural standards ridiculing
the meaninglessness of the modern world.

               CHICARELLI'S MOM
That's nice . . .
          (To Val)
So, whatcha workin' on with the kids here?

                    VAL
A jigsaw puzzle, and it is so totally hard!

Chicarelli's Mom looks it over.

               CHICARELLI'S MOM
I can't even tell what it is!

                    VAL
I know! I've been totally laboring over
this like Boy George at the Estée Lauder
counter for, like, hours!

               CHICARELLI'S MOM
Well, let's get some help --
Mr. Boondoggle! Could you help us with this
puzzle?

               MR. BOONDOGGLE
Sure, girls.

Chicarelli's Mom giggles coyly at being called a girl.

Mr. Boondoggle looks the table over.

                    MR. BOONDOGGLE (CONT'D)
          Say, what's this puzzle supposed to be,
          exactly?

                    VAL
          The box has a cartoon tiger. But I just
          can't see it, and it's rilly hard -- I
          can't even find two pieces to fit together
          to get started, and I'm like totally
          frustrated to the max!

                    CHICARELLI'S MOM
          It's already stressing me out!

                    MR. BOONDOGGLE
          Now, now, relax, and we'll just put all the
          Frosted Flakes back in the box.
                    (Holds up the cereal box)
          I think Ms. Alfie's special presentation
          for this afternoon is about to start. In
          the meantime, you can do me a favor --
                    (Pulls out a sack of M&Ms)
          -- and sort these M&Ms into alphabetical
          order for me.

He walks away, literally leaving them holding the bag. Chicarelli's
Mom drops the sack on the table, takes a handful, and leads Val off
to find a seat.

                    CHICARELLI'S MOM
          Y'know, I hate making chocolate chip
          cookies with these.

                    VAL
          Yah, the floor always ends up, like,
          totally covered in all the gnarly little
          shells!

                    CHICARELLI'S MOM
          By the way, honey, have you ever . . .
          considered . . . oh, I don't know, perhaps
          trying out updating your look, just a
          little?

                    VAL
          Gag me with a spoon, no way! I've rocked
          this awesome look since birth!

She holds up an ULTRASOUND with the adult character's smiling head and leg warmers on it. Chicarelli's Mom shrugs.

>                     MR. BOONDOGGLE
>                 (Aside)
>         You know, I've seen some perfectly adorable
>         baby pictures in my time. And that's not
>         one of 'em.

The rest of the kids and adults start taking seats in chairs and on the floor.

>                     MS. ALFIE
>         Son of a beesting! Where are they?

>                     UNCLE HUGGO
>         You mean today's presenters?

>                     MS. ALFIE
>         Yes! They're supposed to be previewing this
>         year's Avery Play for the children!

>                     UNCLE HUGGO
>         You want me to go look for them for you?

>                     MS. ALFIE
>         Oh, would you? That would be just divine.

>                     UNCLE HUGGO
>         Sure. No problem at all. Stuffy!

>                     STUFFY
>                 (Standing right next to him)
>         Yeah, Uncle Huggo?

>                     UNCLE HUGGO
>         Take a lap around the school and see if you
>         can't locate our lost troop of thespians.

>                     STUFFY
>         Aww . . .

>                     UNCLE HUGGO
>         Hurry along! We're burning daylight!

He turns back to Ms. Alfie. Stuffy pulls a kid aside.

>                     STUFFY
>         Hey kid, I'll give you a dollar to go look
>         around the building for the Avery Play.

>                     KID
>         Sure!

The kid takes off and Stuffy turns back to Uncle Huggo.

                    STUFFY
          Give that kid a dollar for me when she
          comes back.

Uncle Huggo nods and Stuffy exits. Mr. Boondoggle calls Chicarelli
and Woobie aside.

                    MR. BOONDOGGLE
          I told you something was up with those two.
          If there's one thing I've learned looking
          into a shaving mirror every day since I
          turned eleven, it's what a shady character
          looks like!

                    CHICARELLI
          Aw, it's your auspicious mind.

                    MR. BOONDOGGLE
          I'm going to thank you for that even though
          you have no idea what you just said. But
          I'm telling you, there's one reason they've
          left no half-eaten pizza crust or stray
          green bean unturned -- a fortune in gold
          coins!

                    CHICARELLI
          What?

                    MR. BOONDOGGLE
          See, I thought that'd pique the interest
          flickering dimly deep inside that solid
          noggin of yours. We can't let 'em out of
          our sight.

                    CHICARELLI
          And we'll be rich!

                    MR. BOONDOGGLE
          Sure, sure, but to be fair, we'll need to
          put some of it toward Adventure Club, what
          with all the trouble Ms. Alfie's having
          over funding and the budget --

                    CHICARELLI
          Funding! Budgets!

                    MR. BOONDOGGLE
          Shh! Wow, that really is annoying. So,
          Woobie, you're in, right?

>                    WOOBIE
>           I've never seen a good Katherine Heigl
>           movie.

>                    MR. BOONDOGGLE
>           Y'know, that's what I love most about this
>           job: when I finally lose my mind one day, I
>           won't be able to tell the difference.

BETH makes a grand entrance, along with a couple AVERY PLAYERS.

>                    BETH
>           Sorry we're late, but late entrances make
>           everything so much more dramatic, don't
>           they? Ha-ha!

>                    MS. ALFIE
>           Ahh, thank goodness. Now, children, here's
>           the moment you've been waiting for all
>           afternoon: your preview of this year's
>           Avery Play.

Beth shoves a FLYER into Ms. Alfie's hands, taking bows and blowing kisses.

>                    MS. ALFIE (CONT'D)
>                (Reading)
>           "A commemoration of twenty-six years" --
>           twenty-six? Who commemorates twenty-sixth
>           anniversaries?

>                    BETH
>                (From the side of her mouth)
>           Because they missed doing something for my
>           twenty-fifth in the show last year!

>                    MS. ALFIE
>           "The Avery Players proudly present their new
>           production: *Beth! A Celebration in 3-D.*"

The Avery Players pass out 3-D glasses to the kids. They all put them on as Beth struts before them.

>                    BETH
>           Yes, the miracle of 3-D, like James
>           Cameron's epic *Avatar* or Harold and Kumar's
>           Christmas . . . a triumph of technology
>           never before seen on the live stage!

She's swooping in at the kids while the Avery Players also poke things in the viewers' faces. They all jerk and bob their heads to avoid getting hit.

                    BETH (CONT'D)
          Like all great stories, my tale began with
          a breakout role as Conga Dancer Number Four
          in the 1987 Avery production "Splitends"!

                    MR. BOONDOGGLE
                (Yanks his glasses off, disgusted)
          I can't believe they charge five dollars a
          ticket more for this --

                    MS. ALFIE
          Isn't it all spectacular?

                    MR. BOONDOGGLE
                (3-D glasses back on and thrilled)
          -- Especially when they could charge twice
          that and it would still be a bargain!

Beth has her red MISS SCARLET HAT and a huge FEATHERED FAN.

                    BETH
          Miss Scarlet wowed audiences in "Get a
          Clue" --
                (Miss Scarlet voice)
          Ooo, you came from the study? How'd you get
          in there? Are you imported? Ooo, so many
          men, so little time.

She whips off the hat, taking a bow and waving the hat and fan in the
faces of the viewers, including Chicarelli and Woobie.

                    CHICARELLI
          Wow! It's just like everything's coming
          right out at you!

                    WOOBIE
          I got this scar wrestling a monkey at the
          Blacktop Ball.

                    MS. ALFIE
                (Still reading)
          "Only the role of The Lovely Velma really
          shined with the dazzling light she brings
          to the stage!"

Beth flings off her coat to reveal her SEQUINED GOWN and flops a
BLONDE WIG crookedly on her head.

                    BETH
                (Striking a Lovely Velma pose)
          Hold that prize!

>               BETH (CONT'D)
>          (Dropping the character)
>      And this year, kids, we've got a special
>      celebrity guest star I know you kids will
>      all just love!

JUSIN BIEBER strolls in, cool, flipping his hair out of his eyes.

>               BETH (CONT'D)
>      Justin Bieb --

Screaming and cheering cuts her off.

Still cool, Justin Bieber flips his hair again, but his entire HEAD OF HAIR flies off, leaving him completely bald. He screams like a little girl and runs off.

>               BETH (CONT'D)
>      That reminds me --

The CURLY CHORUS bumbles in, taking their places.

>               BETH (CONT'D)
>          (Dropping the character)
>      -- Enjoy this preview of my favorite
>      stooges: The Dads!

MUSICAL NUMBER:

A dance performance to "The Curly Shuffle"

Their dance ends in a chaotic pie fight that spills into the audience with two Curlys chasing each other.

One runs up an aisle as DR. SMITH gets up. As the real principal turns, the second Curly "accidentally" gets him in the face with a pie!

>               MS. ALFIE
>      Well, I'm sure everyone can't wait to see
>      the whole show now! Thank you all so much
>      for the lovely presentation!

Beth, the Avery Players, and the Curlys exit as parents show up and take the kids.

The Writer strolls across stage. Stuffy throws her hands up then gives the writer another $5. He pockets it and exits.

> UNCLE HUGGO
> What was it this time?

> STUFFY
> Aww, I bet him before the show that, with
> all the Marx Brothers, Hope & Crosby, and
> Abbott & Costello routines, there was <u>no</u>
> <u>way</u> they could cram the Three Stooges in,
> too.

> MS. ALFIE
> After all that, I need a vente mocha latte
> soy double-espresso mojito right about now!

She exits. Only Uncle Huggo, Stuffy, Mr. Boondoggle, Chicarelli, and
Woobie are left. Stuffy pulls out the folded map and waves it at
Uncle Huggo.

> STUFFY
> (To Uncle Huggo)
> As soon as we can lose the crumbsnatchers
> and their chief crumb, we can get back to
> searching!

Stuffy sticks the map in her back pocket. Chicarelli sneaks behind
Stuffy.

> UNCLE HUGGO
> Leave it to me. Say, Boondoggle old boy,
> why don't you whisk the kiddies home and
> take off yourself? You look a might peaked.
> Stuffy and I can close shop after we tidy
> up a bit --

Chicarelli grabs the map from Stuffy's back pocket.

> CHICARELLI
> Starting with your treasure map?!?

> STUFFY
> Hey! Gimme that back, you four-foot felon!

> MR. BOONDOGGLE
> Thought you'd take it all for yourselves,
> right?

Chicarelli, playing keep away from Stuffy, backs too close to
Uncle Huggo, who snatches the map back.

> CHICARELLI
> Hey!

> UNCLE HUGGO
> Is for horses.

He holds the map up over his head as Chicarelli jumps unsuccessfully for it.

> MR. BOONDOGGLE
> Let me tell ya, if you're not careful,
> she's gonna find a great big box, climb up
> on it, and sock you right in the knee!

Chicarelli tires and stops jumping.

> UNCLE HUGGO
> The smart biggies always beat out the
> little nasties.

Uncle Huggo pockets the map. Woobie grabs the map from his pocket and runs to the other side of one of the tables.

> WOOBIE
> Yoo-Hoo calls to me.

Stuffy chases her around the table. Chicarelli joins the chase, then Uncle Huggo and Mr. Boondoggle, until all five of them are all chasing in a circle around the table and shouting.

Mr. Boondoggle starts to get tired. He steps out of the chase and leans against a chair.

> MR. BOONDOGGLE
> I need a breather.

He watches the others race around.

> MR. BOONDOGGLE (CONT'D)
> (Aside)
> My money's on the little one to place.

Uncle Huggo starts to slow. The kids and Stuffy actually lap him. Mr. Boondoggle waves him over.

> MR. BOONDOGGLE (CONT'D)
> Say, Huggo, I'm tired, so I know you must
> be.

Uncle Huggo steps out of the chase too. The other three keep going, shouting and running and not noticing Mr. Boondoggle and Uncle Huggo standing together.

> UNCLE HUGGO
> Not as young as I used to be.

> MR. BOONDOGGLE
> Who is? It happens when you live long
> enough. Say, can't complain about the
> weather this year, though.

UNCLE HUGGO

Mild winter like this, can't complain at
all.

MR. BOONDOGGLE

No, not at all.
        (Big sigh)
So, tell me about this map.

UNCLE HUGGO

Stuffy and I got hold of it when we escaped
some river pirates.

MR. BOONDOGGLE

The Deer Creek ones? I hear they can't find
their own bandanas with both hands and a
GPS unit.

UNCLE HUGGO

That'd be the ones.

MR. BOONDOGGLE

And it leads to a treasure?

UNCLE HUGGO

Right under this cafeteria.

MR. BOONDOGGLE

Well, I'll be. Listen, why don't we handle
this like adults.

UNCLE HUGGO

We're the only two in the room.

MR. BOONDOGGLE

If it's a pirate treasure like in every
movie I've seen, there's bound to be enough
for everybody, right?

UNCLE HUGGO

And depending on how much it is, we may
need help carrying it all.

MR. BOONDOGGLE

Fifty-fifty out of the question?

UNCLE HUGGO

We have done all the work so far.

MR. BOONDOGGLE

Well, I had to ask. How about seventy-
thirty, then?

UNCLE HUGGO
I think we could work with that.

MR. BOONDOGGLE
(Shaking his hand)
Excellent. Excellent. I suppose we'd better
be getting back to it.

UNCLE HUGGO
I suppose so.

Mr. Boondoggle gestures for him to go first. Uncle Huggo starts
forward.

MR. BOONDOGGLE
Age before beauty!

Uncle Huggo pauses.

UNCLE HUGGO
Pearls before swine!

He jumps back into the chase around the table, shouting again.
Boondoggle watches for a Beat.

MR. BOONDOGGLE
Well, Geronimo!

He jumps back into the chase around the table too, everyone running
and shouting.

END SCENE 2.


COMMERCIAL #2

ANNOUNCER
"Shenanigans!" will continue, right after
this.

SOUND EFFECTS: SPANISH GUITAR MUSIC comes up.

ANNOUNCER
His personality is so magnetic, he is
unable to carry credit cards . . . Even
Avery parents who don't know him list him
as an emergency contact for their children.

THE MOST INTERESTING MAN IN WEBSTER GROVES ambles in front of the
curtain, cool and adored and knowing it.

ANNOUNCER (CONT'D)
Bear hugs are what he gives bears.

The Most Interesting Man in Webster Groves tips his hat to the
audience.

>                    ANNOUNCER (CONT'D)
>           He was once abducted by aliens, who asked
>           him to probe them. He is . . . the Most
>           Interesting Man in Webster Groves.

>                    THE MOST INTERESTING
>                    MAN IN WEBSTER GROVES
>           I have lived many places in the world. But
>           of them all, the place I call home is
>           Webster Groves. (Beat) Stay Webster-y, my
>           friends.

He steps behind the curtain and exits.

>                                        END COMMMERCIAL.


SCENE 3:

The Avery Cafeteria, empty and dimly lit. Stuffy and Uncle Huggo
sneak in.

>                    STUFFY
>           I still can't believe you made a deal with
>           them, Uncle Huggo!

>                    UNCLE HUGGO
>           Life's about compromise, Stuffy, compromise!
>           It was either that or play ring-around-the-
>           rosy at that table 'til midnight. And you
>           know that's way past my bedtime.

>                    STUFFY
>           Well, I guess you got a point.

She pulls out the map.

>                    STUFFY
>           So, you think we'll find it tonight?

>                    UNCLE HUGGO
>           We better find it soon -- those Adventure
>           Club teachers we replaced won't stay on sick
>           leave forever. Say, did you hear something?

>                    STUFFY
>           Someone's coming! Quick, hide!

>                    UNCLE HUGGO
>           I'll hide in the closet!

>                    STUFFY
>           But --

                    UNCLE HUGGO
        In case you get in any trouble for being
        here after hours. I'll be able to keep an
        eye out for you.

                    STUFFY
        Good thinking! That's using the space
        between your ears for more than storage!

Uncle Huggo ducks into the closet.

                    UNCLE HUGGO
        Lemme just squeeze in here.

                    STUFFY
        Wait -- did you say trouble?

Uncle Huggo closes the closet door. Stuffy dashes over to it and
taps on the door.

                    STUFFY (CONT'D)
        What kind of trouble can we get in?
        Uncle Huggo?

Mr. Boondoggle and Chicarelli sneak in.

                    CHICARELLI
        I still can't believe you made a deal with
        them, Mr. Boondoggle!

                    MR. BOONDOGGLE
        It was either that or watch you two play
        Kentucky Derby all night with Huggo's
        niece . . .

Woobie rushes in suddenly behind them. She darts across the room and
starts running in circles around the table again.

                    MR. BOONDOGGLE (CONT'D)
        Ah, Woobie, glad you could join us.

Woobie stops circling and jogs over to him.

                    MR. BOONDOGGLE (CONT'D)
        -- so what's your excuse for being late this
        time? Lego avalanche trap you in your room?
        Talking ninja lemurs kidnap you to Kirkwood?

                    CHICARELLI
        Ewww . . . don't say that! It's scary!
        Totally creeps me out!

                    MR. BOONDOGGLE
        I had no idea you had such a fear of Legos
        and lemurs --

                         CHICARELLI
              No --Kirkwood!

She shudders and so does Mr. Boondoggle. Woobie nods with big head
motions. Stuffy steps forward.

                         STUFFY
              Oh, it's you all.

                         MR. BOONDOGGLE
              Are we ready to start? Where's your uncle?

                         MR. VON MOLDY (OS)
                    (Singing)
              . . . it won't be a stylish marriage, I
              can't afford a carriage --

                         MR. BOONDOGGLE
              He's probably still leaving for the day!

                         STUFFY
              Quick, hide!

Stuffy and Chicarelli duck behind tables. Mr. Von Moldy enters,
oblivious.

                         MR. BOONDOGGLE (CONT'D)
              Woobie, handle this.

Woobie salutes eagerly and runs to the interim principal.

                         MR. VON MOLDY (OS)
                    (Singing)
              -- But you'll look sweet, upon the seat of
              a bicycle built for two . . .

                         WOOBIE
              Setting the circus tent on fire was an
              accident!

                         MR. VON MOLDY
              Oh, hello child! Isn't it late for you to
              be here?

                         WOOBIE
              I take special vitamins.

                         MR. VON MOLDY
              This time of day, with the lights off . . .
                    (Looking at his watch)
              Or is school about to start?

Woobie leads him toward the closet.

                    WOOBIE
        Emus have wings they don't use!

                    MR. VON MOLDY
        I lose track . . . At my age, it's hard to
        tell what time of day it is sometimes.

Woobie opens the closet door and lets Mr. Von Moldy shuffle in.

                    WOOBIE
        Mashed potatoes feel good between your
        toes.

She shuts the door on Mr. Von Moldy.

                    STUFFY
        Good work, Woobie! It'll be hours before he
        can turn around and get out of there!

                    MR. BOONDOGGLE
        I was more worried that I was starting to
        follow their conversation!

Val wanders in.

                    VAL
        Hey, Mr. B!

                    STUFFY
        Quick, hide!

                    MR. BOONDOGGLE
        There's more people here now than when the
        school's open!

                    VAL
        What are you doing here so late?

                    MR. BOONDOGGLE
        Oh, this 'n that . . . what are you still
        doing here?

                    VAL
        Left my Walkman --

                    STUFFY
        I think someone's coming! Quick, hide!

                    MR. BOONDOGGLE
        Val, have I ever shown you the other side
        of this door?

He takes her by the arm and heads for the closet.

                    VAL
        Uh, no --

                    MR. BOONDOGGLE
          You should really take a look, it's
          quite --

He pushes her in and closes the door as Beth struts in.

                         BETH
          Where's the rehearsal?

                    MR. BOONDOGGLE
          Right this way . . .

He opens the closet door. Beth stalks in and he shuts it.

                        STUFFY
          That was easy.

                    MR. BOONDOGGLE
          It's actually starting to get kinda fun.

Woobie waves at them and just walks right in the closet.

                  CHICARELLI'S MOM (OS)
          Pookie bear!

                    MR. BOONDOGGLE
          We're going to run out of cast members
          soon.

                      CHICARELLI
          She can't catch me here -- I'll be grounded
          for a-turtle-knee!

                        STUFFYY
          Quick, hide!

Chicarelli dashes for the closet. Chicarelli's Mom enters.

                   CHICARELLI'S MOM
          Oh, hi there! Have either of you seen my
          little pookie-bear? She's out way past her
          bedtime and I can't find her anywhere!

Stuffy and Mr. Boondoggle both point at the closet.

                CHICARELLI'S MOM (CONT'D)
          Thanks a bunch! Pookie!

She goes in the closet and closes the door behind her.

A PIZZA GUY shows up, two giant PIZZA BOXES in hand.

                      PIZZA GUY
          I got a double cheese, and a salami and
          onion with extra onion.

                    STUFFY
          There must be some mistake.

                    MR. BOONDOGGLE
          Yes -- this a school, and no one's here at
          this hour--

                    CHICARELLI (OS)
          Those are mine!

She runs out of the closet and takes the pizza boxes.

                    STUFFY
          Who were you planning on sharing all that
          with -- the fifth grade?

                    CHICARELLI
          I was hungry.

                    MR. BOONDOGGLE
          You gonna pay for those?

                    CHICARELLI
          I put 'em on your credit card.

He pats at his coat, pulls his wallet. She waves him off.

                    CHICARELLI
          I got the number memorized.

                    STUFFY
          Oh, and your mom's looking for you.

                    CHICARELLI
          Haven't seen her . . .

Stuffy points at the closet, confused.

                    CHICARELLI (CONT'D)
               (Listening)
          Shh! I hear footprints!

                    STUFFY
               (Bored with it now)
          Quick, hide.

Chicarelli hands the boxes back to Pizza Guy. His hands full, she
shoves him ahead of her as she runs him and herself into the closet.

                    MS. ALFIE (OS)
          Hello! Who's out there?

                    MR. BOONDOGGLE
          It's Ms. Alfie! I'll handle her. Quick, get
          in the closet.

He hustles Stuffy to the closet.

>                    MR. BOONDOGGLE
>           Now, stay in there, and don't come out
>           until I tell you it's safe!

Ms. Alfie walks in, peering through the darkness, barefoot with
COTTON BALLS between her toes.

>                    MS. ALFIE
>           What's it coming to when a girl can't even
>           take a few minutes at the end of the day to
>           do her nails? Oh, Mr. Boondoggle!

She tries to hide her feet, like she's embarrassed.

Mr. Boondoggle struggles to cram the closet shut. She notices.

>                    MR. BOONDOGGLE
>           Ah, Ms. Alfie! Just the delightful
>           personality I was looking for. Some things
>           have come to my attention I think you
>           should know about.

>                    MS. ALFIE
>           Something in that closet?

>                    MR. BOONDOGGLE
>           No, of course not -- why would you ask?

>                    MS. ALFIE
>           Mr. Boondoggle, I mind grade school
>           children every morning and afternoon, and I
>           think I know a dissembling line of hooey
>           when I hear one!

She marches across the cafeteria to the closet.

>                    MS. ALFIE (CONT'D)
>           Now, are you going to tell me about this,
>           or should I just open the door?

>                    MR. BOONDOGGLE
>           You should probably just see for yourself.

He puts his fingers in is ears and squeezes his eyes shut as she
flings open the closet to find --

-- nothing.

>                    MS. ALFIE
>           I -- I'm sorry I doubted you,
>           Mr. Boondoggle. I've had a very long
>           day --

                    MR. BOONDOGGLE
          Oh, I can't even trust me with the change I
          get back when I buy a cup of coffee. Now,
          if you'll step outside with me, I'd like to
          fill you in on some things. . .

They exit. Then the closet door flies open and everyone spills out
and tumbles in a pile on the floor.

                                              END SCENE 3.


SCENE 4:

Mr. Boondoggle and Ms. Alfie in front of the curtain.

                    MR. BOONDOGGLE
          So you see, all we have to do is find the
          treasure, and everybody's problems will be
          solved!

                    MS. ALFIE
          I don't know. It all seems very irregular.

                    MR. BOONDOGGLE
                (Not buying it himself)
          It's for the kids. Say 'yes.'

                    MS. ALFIE
          No!

                    MR. BOONDOGGLE
          I'll take that as a 'yes!'

He takes her by the wrist and starts off.

                    MS. ALFIE
          But I have only nine toes done!

                    MR. BOONDOGGLE
          You'll be able to pay someone to paint the
          other three after we find the treasure.
          Come on!

                                              END SCENE 4.


SCENE 5:

The curtain opens.

Stuffy, Chicarelli, and Woobie are brushing themselves off.

                    STUFFY
          Thought we'd never get rid of all those
          people!

> UNCLE HUGGO
> Why don't you two go bring in the tools
> Stuffy left on the blacktop?

Chicarelli, and Woobie dash off just before Mr. Boondoggle leads in Ms. Alfie.

> MR. BOONDOGGLE
> All right, everybody, Ms. Alfie's in!

> STUFFY
> (To Uncle Huggo)
> It's coming out of their share, right?

> UNCLE HUGGO
> (To Stuffy)
> Oh, yeah.

> MS. ALFIE
> I should have known you two were behind
> this!
> (To Uncle Huggo)
> You're no legionnaire –
> (To Stuffy)
> -- and you're no proctologist! Why would
> you ever come up with something like that?

Uncle Huggo takes out the map.

> STUFFY
> Isn't it obvious? Uncle Huggo, tell 'em,
> why I did it.

> UNCLE HUGGO
> (Studying the map)
> Because Stuffy's a boob.

> STUFFY
> Thanks for clearing that up.

> UNCLE HUGGO
> (Reading the map and pointing)
> So, we've got it figured that the treasure
> must be under the floor or in the walls here.
> Stuffy found a small stash of coins right
> there, so given the underlying structure and
> how the building's settled . . . we should
> probably look . . . here!

He looks up at the closet door.

                    STUFFY
          We'll have to break through the back wall
          of the closet and start digging!

                    MS. ALFIE
          Demolish the wall? Oh, hell --

She spots Chicarelli and Woobie returning with the shovels, etc.

                    MS. ALFIE (CONT'D)
                  (Suddenly bright, with a
                  teeth-gritting smile)
          -- lo! Why are there children here?

                    MR. BOONDOGGLE
          Kids are the best at tearing up schools!

                    MS. ALFIE
          I don't know about this, even if we can
          save Adventure Club!

Ignoring her, Stuffy picks up a hammer.

                    STUFFY
          We're too close to quit now!

Stuffy goes in the closet.

SOUND EFFECTS: Hammering -- once, twice, three times --

Stuffy jumps out of the closet.

                    STUFFY
          Uh-oh!

                    UNCLE HUGGO
          Stuffy, what'd you find back there?

                    STUFFY
          Not quite pirate treasure --

                    CAPTAIN BLACKPATCH (OS)
          Aaarr! Trying to steal our gold, eh?

CAPTAIN BLACKPATCH and a pirate crew spring from the closet, armed
with swords!

                    STUFFY
          Just pirates!

                    CHICARELLI
          But wait -- why would they be hiding in
          there? Why wouldn't they use whatever
          tunnel they came through and just leave
          with the treasure?

MR. BOONDOGGLE
There you go, pointing out every little
thing and ruining the show for everybody!

MS. ALFIE
Now wait just a minute -- are you <u>real</u>
pirates?

CAPTAIN BLACKPATCH
<u>Are</u> we?

MUSICAL NUMBER:

The pirates sing a sea shanty.

As the pirates wind down their song, Woobie sneaks off and returns
with her photo cutout, placing it next to Chicarelli before running
behind the pirates.

The Captain points his sword at the group.

CAPTAIN BLACKPATCH
Gonna take our treasure? Well, we'll take
yours instead! Har-har-har!

Woobie reaches in the captain's pocket, unnoticed, and hands off a
handful of MONEY to Stuffy.

The Captain turns to Stuffy and points his sword. Stuffy immediately
hands over the money Woobie gave her.

CAPTAIN BLACKPATCH (CONT'D)
Let's see -- ten dollars and four gold
coins!

He pockets it. Woobie takes it out and hands it to Uncle Huggo as the
Captain turns to him.

CAPTAIN BLACKPATCH (CONT'D)
Now you!

Uncle Huggo hands over the money.

CAPTAIN BLACKPATCH (CONT'D)
Ahhh, ten dollars and four gold coins. Same
as her!

UNCLE HUGGO
We're on the same pay scale here.

The Captain pockets it. Woobie takes it out and hands it to
Mr. Boondoggle as the captain turns to him. Boondoggle sticks his
hand out immediately and the captain takes the money.

> CAPTAIN BLACKPATCH
> And what do we have here? Ten dollars
> and three -- oh no, there's four -- four
> gold coins. Funny, that's exactly how
> much I have on me today!

> MS. ALFIE
> It's an amazing world of coincidence!

The Captain pockets it. Woobie reaches in again, but this time the
Captain notices.

> CAPTAIN BLACKPATCH
> Say, what's the big idea?

Woobie immediately hugs him, and the Captain drops his sword as he
tries to wriggle free. Chicarelli grabs up the weapon.

> CHICARELLI
> All right, now you hand it over!

> MR. BOONDOGGLE
> I always knew this is how she'd end up!

The Captain gets free of Woobie. He holds out a hand, and one of the
pirates puts another sword in it.

> CAPTAIN BLACKPATCH
> Tough kid, eh?

> CHICARELLI
> Not really. It's actually more of an
> attention-getting device, combined with
> overcompensation for the lack of a strong
> male figure in my life since my parents --

He hits her sword with his.

Chicarelli, scared, hands the blade over to Stuffy.

> CHICARELLI (CONT'D)
> Stuffy!

> STUFFY
> I'm a lubber not a fighter, remember?
> Uncle Huggo!

She shoves the sword at Uncle Huggo who immediately tosses it to
Mr. Boondoggle.

> UNCLE HUGGO
> Boondoggle!

Mr. Boondoggle watches it clatter to the floor in front of him.

> MR. BOONDOGGLE
> Ain't happenin', chief.

Woobie snatches it up.

> WOOBIE
> Woobie!

She and the Captain fence, Woobie expertly, easily, countering everything he does . . .

. . . until she finally knocks the weapon from his hand and points hers at him.

> CAPTAIN BLACKPATCH
> Oooh, please, I beg ya -- I'm not bad, I
> just never had any worthwhile afterschool
> activities to keep me out o' trouble!

> PIRATE
> None of us did!

Mr. Boondoggle snatches up the sword on the floor and waves it crazily, sidling next to Ms. Alfie.

> MR. BOONDOGGLE
> Nobody move or you'll taste the cold steel
> of my rapier! That goes double for you in
> the big feather hat!

> MS. ALFIE
> I think I know a good use for the treasure
> you ruffians absconded with! And what are
> you all doing tomorrow at three o'clock?

> PIRATE
> Ya mean it?

Ms. Alfie nods.

> CAPTAIN BLACKPATCH
> The main reason we became pirates was that
> we were all between jobs!

Woobie tucks her sword in her belt and hugs the Captain.

> WOOBIE
> Say it! Don't just drive around the house
> in the little clown car!

Woobie's not letting go.

Chicarelli's counting gold coins in her hand.

CHICARELLI

Six, eleven, thirty-one --

PIRATE

I think you missed a couple.

CHICARELLI

And so did your face!

CAPTAIN BLACKPATCH

Aw, it'll be fun ta look after kind lil'
children like this!

UNCLE HUGGO

Well, Stuffy, not the treasure we came for,
but we've made some friends and found some
worthwhile employment.

STUFFY

Yeah, it looks like it's the end of these
shenanigans!

WRITER (OS)

Ahem!

Everybody watches as the Writer strolls across the stage and claims
another $5 from Stuffy.

He turns and walks off.

UNCLE HUGGO

Stuffy you doorknob -- how many bets did
you make with that guy?

STUFFY

He was giving me really good odds!

Everybody shrugs and nods like "yeah, okay."

END SCENE 5.

END ACT TWO.

CURTAIN.

THE END

# ABOUT "THE WRITER"

Patrick Dorsey was an Avery Elementary parent for ten years, and he marks the Avery Plays he wrote and performed in as some of the most fun and creatively satisfying experiences he's had.

As a professional business writer, he's spent his career helping people and businesses tell their stories. A natural storyteller his whole life, he began creating his own books in first grade by stapling together crayoned pages. He is a St. Louis native in all but birthplace and holds a degree in English from the University of Missouri, St. Louis, where he also completed the school's noted Writing Certificate program.

It's only with the publication *4 Avery Plays* and his novel *God's Forge* that he's seen his work published without either a stapler or crayons. Although staplers and crayons were employed liberally in producing the Avery Plays ...

Keep up with his upcoming projects and other news at PatrickDorsey.com.

www.ingramcontent.com/pod-product-compliance
Lightning Source LLC
La Vergne TN
LVHW081327060426
835513LV00012B/1209

9 781939 437334